My dear friends,

Once, or more than once, I've dated girls who lived in big houses with big parents who had big wallets. I was out of my element, of course, having been brought up in a "lesser" income type setting. I would skip out on obligations and even cut out time to write so that I could see her. Mostly because stepping through her gate and onto her property was like walking into another world. That's the kind of money she was the princess of. Dating her was an escape from the trenches of my hells and into the loveliness of her infinite-fueled delusions.

We had dinner with her parents one night, because they wanted to meet this "guy that was stealing their daughter's heart in such an unforgiving way".

When her parents asked me what I did for a living, I told them I'm not actually employed anywhere and that I've never actually really had a job; just a place I'd go to that would exchange money for my efforts until either I found someplace better or I wanted to quit altogether, because sometimes being paid in peace of mind is preferable to green pieces of paper we're told is worth something. But I did say that above all, that I am a writer. And the place of which the longest I've ever had a job, I was fired from for writing a book. After I left that night, her parents probably told her never to talk to me again, which being the classy priss that she was, she obliged. Because I never heard from her again.

I've never agreed with someone's parents more than that night.

And finally, to all the women who have seen me in the rawest of my raws:

....my most profound apologies.

Love, as always,
Dave Matthes

Wanderlust and the Whiskey Bottle Parallel

Poems and Stories

by

Dave Matthes

This book is a work of poetry and philosophy. None of it is to be taken in a literal sense or offensively unless otherwise specifically mentioned. Any resemblances to actual events that occur in exactly the same fashion, any persons, locales, or incidents is entirely coincidental. Any names of actual persons that have been used are used in a purely fictional state. Except for Ernest Hemingway; anything written about Hemingway is in the form of personal opinion belonging to the author.

Printed in the United States by CreateSpace.

Front and Back Cover design by Dave Matthes.

ISBN 10: 1503138739

ISBN 13: 9781503138735

Also by Dave Matthes
available on Amazon

The Slut Always Rides Shotgun
The Passive Aggressors

In This House, We Lived, and We Died
Sleepeth Not, the Bastard
Lockless Doors in the Land of Harsh Angels

The Mire Man Trilogy Book 1: *Bar Nights*
The Mire Man Trilogy Book 2: *Paradise City*
The Mire Man Trilogy Book 3: *Return to the Madlands*
The Mire Man: *The Complete Trilogy*

The Kaleidoscope Syndrome: *An Anthology*
Strange Rainfall on the Rooftops of People Watchers: *Poems and Stories*
EJACULATION: *New Poems and Stories*

CONTENTS

Wanderlust

and the
Whiskey Bottle Parallel

~POEMS~

We are currently in the process of reviewing your demand
she wasn't a bitch, but she knew how I liked my steak
Maybe I could (should?) skip town and find something else
a place where the doors don't lock
and whiskey parallels exist opaque and transparent
and without end
Of course
she held my hand, reminding me of music and afternoon naps
Dreams (nightmares?)
What were dreams
Now that
she's nightmaring
Practicality, *she whispered,* you misused your time, and forgot to inhale

My vocabulary isn't what it used to be;
I've drunk all the words and pissed away their meanings

I think if the world consisted of far less
people,
and significantly more liquor stores,
I'd be a happier piece of shit.
But then if less people existed,
there'd be far less a need for liquor
stores.
All I'd need is some advil and a pound of weed,
and I'd be dandy.

There's writing, and there's shitting.
In the same vein, there is life, and there are shadows that have no purpose at all.

If you write a book, you're seen as an artist.
But if you draw it out through your wrists, you're seen as a sinner....

I don't drink because I want to drink,
or because I have to drink.
I drink because someone's gotta
trust me.
Someone's gotta venture down my throat
and probe all those darknesses
outta me.

Continuing the tradition of the heart
and its ability to keep on
beatin' on
despite the situation on the
other side
of the
ribcage
I've decided that a doctor-prescribed
philosophy
is nothing to be fooled around with,
but everything to be fought against;
I still have more scum on my plate
and a few more songs to play
before it's time to turn over to the B-Side
of her

There isn't a single mention of whiskey
not once
in any embrace I might have touched
I only touched it because it was there
and not because I wanted it
I knew that sometime down the road
when the road split in two
or the road fell off the edge
that I'd need a memory
an intangible comfort
something to stop the blood
from flowing
in the opposite direction
spilled and dried
in the land where no bandages reside

I served a brief time in the military
once
soon after realizing life had
nothing left to offer
I ventured to return
and I fought to return
but on the cusp of an eve of that return
I met a woman
I decided to stay and suck the life from her bones
She turned out to be the devil,
of course,
as personified sure-things do,
but she saved me from a certain death
at the hands of the government
and self-despair
so for that alone I am grateful
for that alone,
I'll always remember her
And if not for her,
each of whatever I write
would be at the very least
one chapter light

They would come over in great lines
like a circus
all of them wanting to perform
they would let me fuck them
only to be remembered in some way
because only I could immortalize them
in such a way
that memories never die
but mostly because
they knew only I could remember them
in a way that would define them
they fucked me because
they wanted to know themselves better
my cock was their answer
my sex was their finale
And I redefined them all
it was only until after those nights
that I realized they hated me
because I saw them for who they really
are
creatures of the mind
inhabitants of nothingness
and employees of disaster
what a fiasco those nights were
what unanswered questions
still remain
I guess that's the funny part
I can remember the spaces they filled
their blip on my timeline
but that I can't even remember their names
in a world where names are only names
and nothing else

He held a gun aimed for my gut
saying that he wanted what I had
I told him I had nothing
nothing worth more than
what a nice wad of toilet paper could wipe away
he shot me anyway,
and as he left
he told me I'd never see football season again
I'd never take another bite of warm apple pie
or juicy steak
I'd never write another word
and claim that it was mine to speak
"Make no mistake," he said, "you and I are at war now."

I've only had one beer today
and I'd like another
but the wine is calling me
the whiskey is ever-caressing
All I want is a beer, I said
All I want is a fix
Can't I just get one little fix?
Nope.
No fuckin' way, kid.

He hadn't consumed the food yet
but he was watching us
waiting for us to turn
his fears wanting to be realized
before we were given the chance to turn
he ran
he passed off his bag to me and said
here, you eat them, you're better at being a monster
and so I feasted
In the morning,
I found my clothes
I found my wine
and I drove home
I started over
and he was just his same old self
what a chicken shit.

When the war was going on out east
I was back here in the west
drinking in their drinks
shitting out their tunes
I was part of the machine
the machine that would make animals
of us all if it could
collared animals
beasts with only masters
but I escaped
I made my own escape
No war would ever make an animal out of me

The drugs were only the start
or at least they pretended to be
she came much later
stronger and harder
than anything I'd ever swallowed
she took a hold of me and made promises with her eyes
and I believed them
I still believe them
because they are the only truths that survived
they outlasted the others
and continue to make butchers out of my breaths

It wasn't until I realized
that everyone else would live on
after I died
that death suddenly became a little scary
I'm fine with dying
I'd be ready for it tomorrow
It's 3:43 a.m.
I'd be just fine with an eviction at 4
I'd be okay if there was no Heaven or no Hell,
life is Hell enough and only Heaven when we sin for it
I'm ready right now if the scythe-wielding, black-cloaked
she-demon wants me
If I were to blink and never blink again,
I'd be satisfied with having endured a full life
full of things most people dream about having
but why
after I die
does everyone else get another day to fuck shit up?
I think my problem now
is not that I drink so much
or that I eat so much processed food
or that I masturbate into the toilet so much
but that I'll always think I deserve another chance,
another day to fuck shit up.

Finding someone who has an imagination
is a rarity anymore
Everyone seems to be made out of black holes
always wanting others to fill in the blanks for them
lazy fucking shits
I
have been born a special way
I was designed in a different manner
I am
a black hole
I consume all that I see
I endure it, and eat it up
Not out of choice, you see
but out of necessity
It's something I have to do
I can't unsee anything
I can't regurgitate
all there is for me
is consumption
I am obsessed with the art
the creation
and ongoing quest
for disintegration
I am the hole
I am the empty hunger
the unlimited limit

Birds fly south
and I do too,
especially in bed
when I'm on top
of you

shit yea, I'm angry
hatred is a pretty underrated emotion these days

I'm angry the clocks need to be set back,
as if I really want more time of this shitrock earth

I'm angry I found God,
and discovered he was a narcissist
even more than myself, because I hate competition

I'm angry that my underwear rarely fits anymore

I'm angry my math teachers in high school thought I'd
never amount to anything

I'm angry that niggers, cunts, and faggots are words that
only exist because those people need them to in order to
make a point

I'm angry that this beer is almost empty

Yea, it might sound like I'm bitching
but really I'm just being honest
honesty is a pretty underrated emotion these days

They've all become hypnotized
by Gods and politicians and smartphone apps
And I'm just over here enjoying
this perfect glass of whiskey.

Alcohol has always been my favorite kind of company;
it isn't mean to me until it comes time to shit it all out.
And by that time all I can do
is sympathize with it.

if you don't love your own ass, even when it's in the middle of a nice poo-textured downpour, no one else will.

I met a girl once
she had a stinky snatch
I fucked her anyway
because that was the kinda shit I was into
and now I regret it
not because I've been tainted
because I haven't,
but because, really,
who the hell wants a stinky snatch on their résumé?

Man, I remember when I was a kid.
I used to ignore the cool kids and go out into the woods by myself.
No matter how cold or wet it was.
I was lucky to have grown up in a neighborhood surrounded by trees.
It was in those woods that I think I began to define myself and start to accept the fact that one day I wouldn't be a kid anymore.
Fuck.

I opened her drawer
and found the rubbers
she was still holding her glass of wine
even though it was empty
naked and pale under the lava lamp glow
"I love your writing," she said, touching her clit
"Anything for the fans," I grinned.
Fuck.

At one time
she was important to me
she used to say things to me no one else did
or things no one else had the courage to
I told her to move on
because my road had finally
split in two
and I decided to take the road never travelled by
and so she disappeared
like the last drink I swallowed
an empty glass
a faceless woman
gone off to finish her own adventure
and I was finally at rest

Her tits sagged like wet socks
and her chin felt like sandpaper
she'd propositioned me with those sexy pictures
and I fell for her trap
but I fucked her anyway
I wanted
I needed
I yearned for the cozy, agreeable warmth
between her legs
She had just had the surgery
and so my dick went for a swim
in her swamp
And here I am writing about it
as if she were worth the memory at all
I suppose in fucking her
and allowing her to pay the bill
I let the universe have its way
She was a good kisser, I'll give her that
but I'll never forget those tits of hers
and I'll never forgive them
those floppy, bouncy
cartoons upon her chest
Life's a bitch
and full of false advertisements
I think that was the night I finally
stopped falling for them

I've had numerous brain docs
and people who pretended to give advice
and if there's one thing they all saw eye to eye on
was that I was a jerk
I feel like a great weight has been lifted when I write that
Here's to another night
and another piece of shit poem

I fell into a hole once
I was in the middle of the woods again
It wasn't until I scratched my balls the next day
that I realized it was a woman all along
Must remember to take a shower after every cunt
words to live by
philosophy to be carved into my grave
you read it here first

I may have had a moment in the past
during my formative years
in which I fell in love with a wall
this wall in particular was smooth where it counted most
curved when the rest of the room demanded so
and where it met the floor, the baseboards
signed a treaty with a pale-green-colored carpet
she wasn't diseased
or untouchable
but she'd had one too many drinks the night before
and three two many pain killers for breakfast
I made that wall cum seven times that night
or so she said
and every framed portrait tacked to her surface
shook and quaked
some fell from their landings
and the glass became embedded in the carpet
but that wasn't the problem
the worst of it was the guilt that infect my veins
Just two days prior,
I'd signed a paper that allowed the contractors
to break down her wall, and uproot her carpet

"I met someone," I said, "I think I'm going to marry her."
The guilt only lasted a week.
Because after all,
she was only a wall.

"Listen," she said

"Please," I begged

And when the sun set
and the moon came out
I slipped inside her
one last time
In the morning I left
A week later
she had a new man
Nothing changes,
though sometimes it does
And so my quest began
I lit my cig
I swallowed my drink
and decided for the rest of my days
they'd all be Me-Days
I've since confronted myself
and destroyed that demon
but I'll never forget her last word:
"Listen"

Lovecraft says he knows about tentacles
but that motherfucker never bedded a girl from
West Chester
and survived

She was a toothache
that one
and she tasted like crack
the best thing about her
was if I was ever hungry
I could always make a meal out of whatever
was making rest at the corners of her mouth
I can't remember her name
as is the case with most of them
then again I can't remember
how many donuts I ate this morning
or how many beers I'll drink tonight,
tomorrow

Her boyfriend
or who used to be her boyfriend
slept in the next room
because the bitch had yet to move out
So we made out on her couch
while Julie Andrews serenaded the goddamn mountains
At the end of the night
I masturbated into the womb of the stars
because she was a fucking Christian
not a Catholic
but a Christian
with hair on her legs and in her pits
and a boyfriend who lived with her
FUCK

Standing in the lunacy fringe
of us

Acquaintances.
Friends.
Lovers.
Haters.
Romance lost, romance traitors.
I loved you, too scared to tell.
Just how much it felt like hell.
Thanks a lot you fucking bitch,
you know just where to make me itch.

I found out today
just by walking up a few flights of steps
that my heart has moved into a particular neighborhood
notorious for making hearts explode
Irony has always played a spear carrier in my play of life
but not today
today
irony rears its hideous cunt head
all the years of ripping out the hearts of women
and finally my own is in line for the guillotine
I'm not dead yet
so maybe soon
It's only November
An arrow through the gut might speed things up
They even told me to stop drinking
Sorry Doc,
but I've still got shit to do
probably not much
but not much is more significant than none at all

I met a man once while in the woods
I suppose he was there for the same reason as I
seclusion
isolation
permeation
meditation
translation perhaps
perhaps he was just wandering
He said to me,
"Obscene, isn't it? How all these trees can grow to be so tall and beautiful...yet here they remain? Never moving where their roots won't allow. They are born here, and they die here."

If he had a point, I'll never know.
The drink has dulled my mind
and deafened the necessary parts of my soul
Maybe that's what he was talking about
Maybe that's why he came to the woods

Deterioration.

I've found
through much silence on my part
that the moments between sleeping
and not sleeping
whether they have substance or
can be remembered at all
those footholds between our ears
tightropes for our most daring handstands
and cartwheels
where most would jump at the chance
for those kinds of adventures
I'd find places they'd all run away from
I wandered among the leftovers
the food restaurants tossed out after everyone else left
the beer at the bottom of the bottle
I was always younger in those dreams
never older
or dying
of decrepit
just
younger

My mother wasn't evil
not by traditional standards
she was more or less an embodiment
of those commercials that suddenly get louder
when the real show isn't on
That's at least what she's become
I miss the old her
the her of which I probably never really knew
When I was six or seven
and not yet eight or nine
I found her at the kitchen table around noon
alone
she was crying
she didn't see me
on her plate was a half-eaten pb and j
to this day
I still have no idea why I found her like that

Around the same time as the half-eaten
pb and j
I'd spend most of my summers in the woods
Once I found a fort
or what had once been a fort
the flooring panels were fallen through
the walls had been soaked through and cracked
even the tree in which it was set had keeled over
Maybe it'd been here for a while
maybe years
maybe decades
but the place was empty
the space was mine
and it was here I'd come when the days were brightest
and also darkest
but once I told my friends about it
my refuge became a badge of unpopularity
they couldn't understand why I liked being alone so much
they said I was crazy
and their parents said I was too young for that nonsense
These days
I'm told I'm too old to want to be alone
When is it ever a good time to want such things?
Maybe that's why I'm dying.
Maybe I need a new place of refuge.

I met the traveler
just as we'd planned
at the crossroads of north and east
just where we'd intended
We shook hands
patted each other's backs
and continued on our way
"Maybe if, we ever get lost," she'd said,
"We can find each other at a familiar place," I replied,
It wasn't a promise
because promises break like glass
glass with no reflection
and we were mirrors,
she and I
mirrors traversing the abyss
"See you soon," she said.
But every mirror fades with time
because I can't even remember what she looks like
anymore

The first thing I ever wrote
was a story about a boy with a pet dinosaur
I called it "My Dinosaur",
Something so impossible,
innocence in the arms of the unattainable,
limitless episodes of danger and friendship and victories
never a single tragedy or failure
and I only ever stopped writing them
when I ran out of paper
and when the homework really began to take over;
it wasn't until recently that I realized
I am still the boy
and my future is still My Dinosaur
but now
I've drunk all my innocence
drunk and fucked it all away
and the unattainable...
...I've met with Death today.
She told me, "Have a seat, we'll be with you shortly."

I've seen a lot of her recently
The Fall
The Spring
The Summer
The Winter
Her
Seasons and gestures
ain't nothin' but lost travelers
forever on the hunt for sustenance
and cherry blossoms
Have you ever seen the pedals of a tree
float to the ground in the dead of winter?
No, but I have looked into the eyes
of many who've loved me.
Oh, so you have.

I am awake
I am without rest
I cannot shut my eyes
Nor can I turn off my heart
I am alive
because to die
is foreign
to live
is dangerous
but it is all I can do for now
I am awake
I am with the moon and the stars
and she is in the bed waiting for me
she is asleep
resting
and I am awake
dying

A woman once told me
"Death has more humanity about him than you or I,
or anyone else for that matter."
I suppose
in the grand scheme of things
scraping off the shit from the bottoms of my boots
and tempting the Gods who decide
who has what kind of heart attack
each day
and not sacrificing my art
for a paycheck
or for the mass-prized love of the masses
I've become Death in a way
It's obvious I need more to drink
I've been staring at the bottom of the bottle so long
I can see my face
all dreary and melty looking
contorting and forming into shapes
that aren't death-like at all.

She wore a pair of leggings
with holes in all the right places
access so easy my seven-incher had no quips
She smoked menthols though
but I didn't mind
like me,
she was a slut for whiskey
and was always ready to fuck
but back in those days
I was always ready to fuck
Now all I care about is the cleanliness of my asshole
and if there's beer in the fridge
Time is a funny thing
Maybe if Time had a pair of leggings
our evolution would slow
and there'd always be time for fucking
and menthol cigarettes
and whiskey
and ink-covered women
But I'm writing this as a man
who's made too many bad choices
In the same way a wanderer thinks he's doing right
by seeking water in a desert
I've sought all the wrong needs
and all the right wants
And now I'm dying of the self
So that not even the self can do anything
any sort of rescuing
Strange, though
as I'm writing this while sitting beneath a tree
I'm starting to think I should have been born a tree
so that the branches would be my only worry
my only facade.
Even when I was a kid
I hated people
I hated being around them
In their big crowds
Lost in their loud gloatings

So I'd spend most of my days
In the woods
I had a stream I'd go to
Where I'd go to catch minnows
I only ever caught one or two in that spot
But the stream only grew narrower
And shallower
In either direction
And that meant even less to find
It was my first lesson in being taught
That it didn't matter which way I went
For the time being at least
I was right where I was supposed to be
It was deep here
And I could still see the sky
There wasn't ever a lot of fish to catch
But at least I wasn't ever bothered by people
And their endless shit
And their fake curiosities
Their fatigued and wearisome lies
It was just me out here
And just me was just fine.
Not much has changed in two decades
I have traded the stream
In exchange for the blank page
And a ceaseless nostalgia
And as before as is now
That's just fine.
The day I became a writer
it wasn't the day a whore paid me in sex
in exchange for one of my books
which happened often and more and more
as time went on
it wasn't the first time someone
actually paid for one of my books
which happens less and less
as time goes on
It was the day I realized

that everything is created by man
God, Satan, Judas, phobias, excrement, even death
even women
everything is created by man
So I said to myself
shit, let me make something
let me tape together some words
and sentences
and prose
and predicates
and the residual shit that sticks to my ass after I wipe
and compose a new kind of thing
But then I realized that others had discovered this
for themselves as well
And suddenly the world became a jungle
Where everyone eats each other alive
And shits out the same shit

And when the headache comes
the following morning
it hits me like a freight train
whose brakes have failed
They will eat you
Chew you into tiny pieces
easier for them to swallow
Sometimes they will be people
who were at one point never hungry
Sometimes they'll be the very people who
shat you out from their cunt
It's these people who will die alone
And it is these people you must kill
before you are killed
I have found there is only one defense
against these demons
these horrors
Sleep
whiskey
a good cunt to shove my cock into
And someone who understands
even if they don't have a face
even if all they are is a glimpse
a glimpse into a dream
a building in the city of distance
out of reach from our hands
but ever in the sights of our eyes
Hope
That is the defense
that is the truth that paves
our final road

In the days when we decided
to stop being children
and start being soldiers
the ground seemed to give way
and the walls grew personalities
They gave us clothes to wear
but we'd feel anything but clothed
We were exposed
We collapsed from the inside out
They took from us our emotions
and replaced them with apathy
But I left
I made my escape
I wasn't taught this
I just sort of knew
Embrace all emotions:
sadness
happiness
sorrow
hate
love
prejudice
fear;
they are weapons
against our greatest enemy:
indifference
The military boys can keep their soldiers
I'll keep my wits
and continue to fight the real fight
the only fight that matters

What busy pretension our bones and limbs must endure
moving and twisting and bending in ways
the mind constantly says no to
but the brain constantly says yes to
Categorically speaking,
to compartmentalize the drones and feces of our endeavors
Endeavoring forevering and starving for moonlight
Here lies those who wandered too far
those who ceased in trepidation
and those who climbed the backs and
stood on the shoulders of the blind
What busy pretension
what useless monocles of untruths we lead
Is it such a thieving transparency to want
a breath more than a bereavement?
I've paid higher taxes and stolen shinier golds
than most
And I've made all the better for it
My kind won't survive
though
because only the greedy survive
And so I drink more
I swallow and consume
and I wait for the blackest angel to scratch my back
because an itch scratched is a stitch hatched.

Fingerprints catacombing glass panes
with a fluctuating timestamp on our time cards
We've delved into the barrows and wastes
and come home dirty each night
A facing wonder
stemming from a plateau of what-if's
and what-could-never-be's
we didn't stop to wonder if upon that land
if we should find not what we wished
but the things that should never be
And so with palpitating hesitation
I step back from the edge
and return to the constance
and the wanton Man who commands us all

Following each glass of impermanence
I chase the sunset with a bottle of wine
not to whine but to see
her eyes and
her hair and
her shadow
shine
I let the embodiment of her ocean carry me off
to places only seen in picture books
Following a path through the pale and grimness
I've never been born before this day
she wrapped her existence around my flesh
and like debris and the wind
we wound together
and faded into nothingness
the nothingness the horizon craves
and in which vacancies wallow.

I can feel her skin
as I thumb through the pages
I can taste her breath and feel it caress my neck
as I smell the fresh ink within
she is my greatest novel
my best work
there is no equal and never shall be
the many chapters of her being
a just and ragged symphony
with a crooked conductor
but she is my music
her notes slipping into through my ears
and down into my bones
she is my best work
my greatest story
a story without end
any end would be less than deserving

I can smell the food downstairs
And the people laughing
My lady's family
And all of their family
I am stuffed but not yet ready
I am drunk but not yet steady
I've had my fill
But I am ongoing
And hungry still
Thanksgiving
And the romance card
Playing one and the same
Until the sun sets
And tomorrow truly kills us all
The food is settled.
I've had my share
And the walls are thin
So thin and bare.
Outside the birds are singing
To their chicks and children.
The trees are black against the ever-paling sky.
And I have written this all
From the comfort and convenience
Of the shitter upstairs.
And yet nothing has come out,
I fear I've eaten too much
So much I've been plugged
Plugged and stalled
It was worth it.
It's always worth it.
If it doesn't hurt in some way
If no pain is had for sin and stay
Then nothing is worth doing
And breathing would have to wait for another day.
I'm sure I'll wake up sometime soon with fright.
And everything I've eaten
Will erupt
And explode out of sight.

So with all of that said,
And my uncompromising constipation
Tucked in to bed,
Happy Thanksgiving to all
And to all a good night

Far from the epoch
of us
glimmering southward
and slightly inbound
it lands without tracks
and promises no storm or quarrel
The beginning has begun
and we will ride the autumn leaves
until the final setting of our winter sun

The Lady knows
And she's already signing letters to the war
We've received them all
but are told of no more's return

Write
Drink
Love
Breathe
Fuck
Fuck
Fuck
Fuck
Fuck
Fuck
Fuck
Fuck
Fuck
Fuck
Fuck
Fuck
Fuck
Fuck
Fuck
Fuck
Fuck
Fuck
Obey the philosophy of the wind.

Ground was broken through
and walls built only with their bones showing
The pillars atop the curvature struck gold
when the sun kissed the sky goodnight
Granting an apologetic grimace
We're all in love with the day
but love the night stronger still
Cold is the starlight
soft is the snowfall
And with the Lady in one hand
I went home
and channeled her into me
I became suffocated by togetherness
and tenderness
and with her in my embrace
I went home

So many people trying to be nots and will never be's
they naught and are fraught all the way down
to their innards
So much so that when they bleed
from the littlest slice
they ooze and ooze and feed themselves
unwillingly to the rats and mice
They are sympathy-proof
those people
and all of them are out there
they're in the streets
tucked in to their lofts
snug and tight beneath the Christmas tree
unfinished and vacant will their tiers stand
and their tears
their tears will freeze into glaciers
and one day will melt as the old ones did
the cycle will repeat and repeat
until we are all drowned
choking and without air
our lungs dysfunctional
and our hearts immobile
A symphony of digression
repressed by aggression
stung and bitten by suppression
Oppression
is the operative word
That and grandiose affairs of wild timidity
soaked with our own little seasonal gifts

They always came in to my room
up the stairs and shutting the door behind them
They came knowing and willing
wanting
curious
or bored
then came their clothes
the floor was a sea of those things
covered by their coverings
And suddenly I'd kiss them
or they'd kiss me
Suddenly further
I slipped inside of them
and they into me
And then the night ended
And I was once again alone with my whiskey
The window would be open
And it didn't matter what kind of air blew through
The music hummed dimly
Or not
And I was once again alone with my whiskey
I would smile and remember
Sometimes I'd call another number
But whether she was one incarnation or the other
The Lady
was always meant to be my always

There aren't as many paths as there were
overgrown probably
vanished and invisible
That place offered so much freedom
and all the time time could give
It was only just behind my house
filled with trees
and hills
and pathways and trails
I can't ever go back
not because it's not there
but because I'm not allowed
I'm a man now
why would I be allowed?

One day
the end of the world will invade our headlines
there will be warnings of imminent doom
perhaps even a deadline beneath the gloom
but the people will riot
the people will mangle each other
and eat one another
until nothing is left
the deadline will pass
and the promise of the end will fade
the world was never meant to end
but the fear
the fear will drive people to burn it
the people
us
we
we will be the cause for the end
because the person is a genius
but people are unintelligible, mindless motherfuckers.

Painted dysentery
splashed upon the mosque
suddenly it's a mausoleum
of turquoises and lavenders
of helium perplexities and ambidextrous anomalies
I've wandered through the valley
of the shadow of death
I've scaled the peaks
of the toothed distances
Now my nose is running
And all I can taste is candlesmoke
Fascist toilets exploding with all the fucking shit
I've just vomited and bled from my mouth
My brain says I'm tasting copper
but all I can taste is candlesmoke
When I was on fire
I was told I brought warmth to the table
to the bedroom
but now it's dark and black
and all she can smell is candlesmoke

Hear that train whistle
off in the distance
I've heard it for years and years
I've also worked a hundred and five
shit jobs
and paid more in due than salary earned
I stabbed myself with a screwdriver yesterday
accidentally
When I saw the blood
seeping slowly at first
rising through the lays of skin
running down my fingers
Until it covered my hand like a glove
I loved that moment
I look forward to the next accidental stabbing
One day, the end of the world will blow out the flames
until our senses are incinerated
until not even the scent of candlesmoke
will voice those whistles
distant in the night

Have a beer
stroke the beard
and ponder life without a motion;
Emotion?
Who needs regrets when you've got
emotion?

I'll be by the bar.
It's nice here
warm and cold
like driving through the dead of winter
windows down
heat blasting through the vents
Something for everyone
I'll be by the bar
because the seats are ripped and torn
but the whiskey is always cold
in glasses of scorn
Hey bartender
leave the bottle, asshole
this beard ain't gonna soak itself

[**STEPS IN**]

There's folly in her stride
that's the rumor
justified by lies
I've seen her up close
beneath the sheets
and sometime during the summer
she was mine for a few sweet months in the fall
and parts of December

To get to the heart of this unsolvable equation, one must first become familiar with the physical, emotional, and immaterial makeup as to what constitutes both war and peace.

I found her looking through a window
the same window I'd been looking through
She smiled and her eyes never faltered
this folly was a crime

The very essence of war is destructive, though throughout the years utilized as a means of creating peace, such an equation might seem paradoxical to the untrained eye. Some might say using evil to defeat evil is counterproductive, and gives more meaning to the word "futile". Others, like Edmund Burke, would argue that "the only thing necessary for the triumph of evil is for good men and women to do nothing."

She had an identity I could identify with
something my fingertips could caress in the night

There is such a limitless landscape within the mind, no two minds are alike. And this is why as a race we will forever be at war with each other.
What constitutes peace is in the mind of the

beholder.

Have you heard the argument?
This displacement of men and women
and women and men
the minds we all have
the beliefs we all share
Slipping inside of us
thoughts and religions and bodies
all bare

"Without darkness, there can be no light," he once said. To demonstrate this theory, during one of his seminars he held a piece of white chalk and drew a line down the center of a blackboard. Explaining that without the blackness of the board, the white line would be invisible.

When she left
she kissed with eyes open
I knew this because I'd done the same
Sometimes we saw eye to eye like that
Very briefly,
she considered an apotheosis
a synthesis
a rendering of her folly
into solidarity

To believe that a world-wide lay down of arms is possible, however, is the delusion of the pacifist; the dream of the optimist; and the joke of the realist. Diplomacy only goes so far, and in spite of our efforts to fight with words- there are times when drawing swords of a very different nature are surely called for.

Experiencing the subsequent sunrise
inhaling and drinking

breaking mirrors and regurgitating
just to start again
all in all
I was just another gash in the bark

Plato once said:
"Only the dead have seen the end of war." Perhaps the death of us all is called for in this time of emotional desperation. War is a product of the mind; only with the death of such will come the end of the bloodshed. Though this may be a fairly realistic view of such an issue, perhaps there is an optimistic outlook on the horizon. Not every sword is double edged, but every coin is double sided.

Leaving town and throwing shit out the window
drinking boroughs and borrowing spare change
I glimpsed the rear view mirror
stole a glimpse really
I've believed in looking back for a while
it helps to have one last view
a reminder in case one ever decides to rebel
in the event the self regresses
and makes the declaration of devastation
once more

Thus, if we wish to eliminate the threat of war today-complete human annihilation may be called for.

[**STEPS OUT**]

I've worked a thousand and one jobs before
this one
And that's fine
I was bound to break eventually
My words don't rhyme anymore
The comma between them do
and the semi-colons scream for narcotic remedies

There; no pleasing everyone
they;re all there because they can be
not because they can;t go anywhere else
Ins;t that what shadows are for?
To remind us of our mustn;ts and wouldn;ts
To bleach our aren;ts
Fuck the bastards who mine
Who take the doorknobs and return the clocks
to their rightful positions
I;m me for a reason
I;m meant to move beyond and through
I;m just as combustible
I;m not in the business of having without wanting

Some people go to shows to hear the music up close
My life is full of tunes
Most I don't care to hear
But lyrical narrations nonetheless
I'll pass on wasting cash
I've got all the musical footnotes I need right here
Turn the cassette over and what
do you have
The other side of life

The tuberculosis has slammed into a wall
My intentions have been repelled
and replete
HELP
HELP
HELP
I was not aware of the infection!
But this one thing
this one illness
is not something one can touch
or erase
or paint over
No
And one never catches it
they must have it
as soon as they exit the womb
One only has it once they discover it
And then they have it for life
Eviscerate me now
I was not aware at all
Though
from time to time
I have been known to lie

Nothing is necessitated by
a will to connect
There is no will in the meet
a moot point, perhaps
mayhaps
a moot logic, absolutely
But I have not seen the sun without first
seeing the stars
I've not tasted the dawn
without embracing the kiss of night
Maybe I'm the ill-will connoisseur
I've stepped in enough shit to afford a manure farm
I could write about that if I wanted to be like
all the rest
a moot meandering

I woke up once
while all the rest were asleep
I heard a muttering
and some mumbling
in the bunk three beds down and across the runway
he sat there with something metal
in his wrist
He saw that I'd seen
the red was thick
and his eyes overshadowed
by grief
He was whispering the eleven general orders
As he bled his rest away
I sympathized
our dreams had been crushed and disintegrated
nothing more than opaque pieces of glass way up
and far away

It doesn't take a genius with a pen
to sign their name on the dotted line
But it does take a child to lie about coloring
inside the lines
connecting the dots
and sharpening their pencil
Maybe next time I'll just buy her some fucking flowers

Whiskey can calm the nerves
or better
Wine can warm the sheets
or harden the stare
Beer can moisten the space
between the legs
I've seen all three in action
I've held a woman once
But sometimes one must divide
and carry the one
One must be the remainder
and as for the consultant on timekeeping
tell him I ran away with his daughter
It's only a mistake if you don't learn from it

Only in looking in a mirror can a man see himself devoid of all exterior demotivation,
PARTITION THE URGES;
seeing a homeless man fixed in the confines of a back alley one can either observe, ignore, or contribute; all of these being acceptable by the general population but only one being the right choice for the individual,
COMPARTMENTALIZE THE WINE;
Does one kill himself because of his conceited self-loathing or for the literal good of society,
SUBVERT THE ADVERSE
FUCK THE TRANSVERSE
DRINK THE OBSERVERS;
But if we choose to not end our life because of society's "laws", who or what then are we succumbing to? If we don't end our lives because of those laws, is it because we feel we don't own our own lives, in which case does society own our lives? So what then would be the "right choice"; is there a "right choice" at all? The collective conscience has said that life is unfair; the truth is far less obscure: it is only when we succumb to fear when life becomes unfair,
EYES BEFELL A MAN ONCE,
AND HE SAID TO ME,
Oh, the tangled webs we weave and yet still we cannot take responsibility; because we are a race of sad forgivers, and cannot bear the thought of our own decisions being the cause of the misery we live in,
I CURSED him AND BELITTLED him
YET HE CONTINUED,
Centuries from now our actions today will be placed in the annuls of historical failures and we will once again succumb to the will of the Universe or madness.
he TOLD ME ONE LAST THING,
he SAID THE MOST IMPORTANT ARTIFACT OF BEING ALIVE
IS TO NOT JUST BREATHE, BUT ALSO
to inhale **(AND THERE WERE ECHOS IN TOW)**

I once masturbated
with so much hair conditioner
the next time I porked a woman
she never called back
later, years down the road
she sent me an apologetic message
"I prefer men with hard, rough cocks."
So now,
when I masturbate,
I use sandpaper.

I don't quite understand
people
who don't turn on the water
before stepping into the shower
do they not think they'll be disappointed
once they realize they've made a mistake
of not thinking ahead?

On a business trip to Tokyo,
I sat with a stranger at a bar
He had pink hair because he'd recently been
shanghaied into a drag queen show
we talked about sequins and horizontal cunts
we talked about remedies for broken hearts
and sniffing glue
It wasn't until the bartender told me he was deaf
that I'd realized I'd been justifying my own delay
I didn't want to go home
Singing into a free microphone
and shooting the shit with strangers
was all I wanted
it was all I had left
My homeward trek
should I decide to take it
would have more in common
with the bottom of a barstool
than the cleavage of a virgin

If you can't decide between beer and wine
best bet is to subtract the two
don't forget to carry the whiskey
and divide by a low-grade narcotic
Then switch on some music
and pretend
like you're the greatest lover
that ever
lived
After you've convinced yourself of this grand lie
and when the fuzziness hits
and the toes go numb
that's when you know you
did it right

Mathematics of Being 101

I took the beer and let it settle at the bottom
of my belly
there it waited
until the whiskey followed
and together they churned into a muck
like a boiling bog
like the swamp behind the house I grew up in
Stirring together, being mixed and saturated with
one another
as my body moved
in a horizontally and vertically
fucking motion
I felt their desperate climb
they wanted to escape
but the woman grasping my throat
kept their contest at bay
fighting fire with fire
her sex always wins
And after she screams
I wander to the toilet
and puke my guts and soul into the bowl
tomorrow I'll start all over again

Soaking through the carpet
I can feel the floorboards quivering
I've gone and done it again
Opened the cell and let everything out
I've taken too much for myself
expunged their passage
and repaved their streets with invisible pathways
[DON'T worry]{don't?}[DO NOT]
Stale beer from the night before is still beer.
Sustenance, it is
Nothing's changed
drink it
And soon you'll remember why you came here
in the first place

my brain has rested
on slabs of boiling hot rock
for longer
and greater stretches of immobility
Than I can or care
to remember
Rembrandt.
They flipped me over to my other side
my sunny side
Told me to hold my breath and close my eyes
When I opened them again
I saw the wreckage
I could smell the flames
And so I drank some more
a lot more
Whiskey isn't so flammable after you piss it all out
And storms on the sea
and the brainsmithing upon the parchment
the canvas
and the sheath
All the pieces want a little bastardizing

There are people who see
Or try to see
Or want you to think they see
the good in other people
I am not one of these
By nature.
I'm sure there is good somewhere
And if there is
Why has it run into hiding?

I lay there
Alone
But flanked by lit candles
And a bottle of red wine.
This was life.
On some nights
Sometimes most
And I loved it.
This was enough for me
Wine
Good smells
Music through my ears
I didn't need to be numbed
This was enough.

Some desperate panache
Despair shoulder to shoulder
Would we be so evil to move
The hands forward an hour
Break the springs
Smash the mattress
Stay on top
Or find someone who would
Murdering certainty
Except for seconds
And thirds
The wealth in your eyes
The warmth in your tributary
I used to write these out by hand
Some things change
Nothing too

Fire in a bottle
A few seconds,
A few hours
It'd never be enough time

And so the general
Said to the general
"We're here at last,
As we suspected we might be"
That's what you said the last time
"Indeed I did, but so did you,
So why not one last drink"
Your congress and your presidency
Is out of control
"No no no,
We have all the control"
But we were friends once
Once we had summers and days off
We cheated on tests and dated the same girls
You saved my life and I saved yours

But the two generals came here for a reason
It's in the hands of us, they both agreed
They drank
And they shook hands
A moment later
They parted.

And never crossed paths again

Someone told me
the cure to the end
is not in finding a new beginning
but in continuing the end
so that the end never comes
That's why I can't look away from her
The Lady

Day writing
and
Night writing
there is a difference
like drunk driving with a friend
laughing and cackling
pointing at assholes
when you stop at green lights
and explode through the red ones
Makes me want to rock and roll
all night long
I heard someone once say
that my behavior was destructive
that my point of view was plague-like
Then why am I still living?
Why am I able to wake up
and grin?
I've lived against their rules
for a long time
and my life
my writing
my women
my panache
has been all the better for it
See, mom?
People love me
despite my own self-loathing
Either that or they love my writing
which is better than the former
And even if they hate it
I've driven emotion from them
in some way
and my life
my writing
my women
my eyesight
has been all the better for it
cheers

"I'd like to quit," said I.
"quit what?" said the man.
"Life."
"Why?"
"Spite."
"Spite?
"It's as good a reason as any. Just hasn't turned out the way I expected."

The man before me stood a hint slouched
his eyes sank into his skull like coals on a beach
He might have been able to be trusted
he had that air about him
as many old men in the dead of night have

"So you stepped out into the storm
and your upset because you got a little wet?" He asked.
"Not wet," I said, showing him a Polaroid from the day before
the gloss shone beneath the moth-surrounded street lamp
their hum matching the bulb's
in admiration and lust
"Drenched and soaked," I rang out my beard,
showing him just how wet I still was

"Well," he said, "I can't just let you in without payment."
I searched my pockets, knowing he'd ask me something
like this
I breathed heavy, hoping I remembered to bring it

"You're breath stinks of wine," he said, "are you sure you're
here
on your own accord?"

My pockets felt empty
and I suddenly realized what had happened.

"She took everything," my voice fell, and the man crossed his arms, "she's taken everything."

Dancing with a bride who wasn't mine
was the best thing I ever did at a wedding
Fuck the heartbreak,
I've got a stolen bride

We are currently in the process of reviewing your request
she wasn't a bitch, but she knew how I liked my steak
Maybe I should (could?) skip town and find something else
a place where the doors don't slam
and whiskey parallels exist freely
and without judgment
Of course
she held my hand, reminding me of music and afternoon naps
Sleep (rest?)
What was sleep
Now that
she's asleep
Practicality, *she whimpered,* you misused your time, and
forgot to inhale

Listen, I just wanted a place to stay
but you've already stayed
you've locked both doors
trapped yourself
me
It was never my intention
if it wasn't your intention
you'd never have turned the knob
in the first place
Maybe it was my intention

Maybe chaos is my coda

~STORIES~

AS WE FORGIVE THOSE WHO TRESPASS AGAINST US

A Short Story

Randall, a homeless man inherits the homestead of his well-off yuppie mother and meets the young girl next store, Astrea. He falls in love...and geriatrics of retardation ensue....

I. Masturbatory Complex

The first time my mother caught me masturbating, I was fifteen years old and having just gotten over the sudden passing of my first dog Zepp. The look on her face was about as shocked as you might be imagining. A better word to describe the contortion-themed facial art would be: mortified. Here was her innocent, fifteen-year old son, someone whom had basically done everything a good boy should have done while growing up including but not limited to: going to church every Sunday, Easter, and Christmas, apologizing when he was wrong, telling the truth even if it was about just telling a lie, complimenting her on her cooking, agreeing with his parents on both of their conflicting political affiliations, always looking both ways before crossing the street, holding the door open for the elderly, even the ungrateful ones, chewing with his mouth closed, and here he was...with his right hand on his fucking cock pumping away to a BBW Redhead aptly named Star Supernovaclit, moaning and screaming away like a nine-year old experiencing her first moon bounce.

It took my father an hour to calm her down and to convince her it was just a phase. My father told me later that he understood my pain of losing Zepp; apparently he was under the impression my masturbatory acts were due to said emotional severance. And so he went on to explain the importance of aiming my masturbatory needs in as positive direction as possible.

"Don't rub em out in vain, son," he said, "trust me on that." My dad liked to wear flannel a lot. I think it's because his father wore flannel a lot. I hated it though, and my father knew that. It had been the subject of many awkward dinner table conversations, especially when the relatives were over. When he bestowed upon me his father-to-son guidance, wearing that flannel the way he did, I imagined him as a lumberjack talking down his greatest oak foe, convincing it that their meeting was destiny...and that the edge of the blade of his ax, would be its savior from this evil world.

My mother combated her newfound knowledge of my vain with increased trips to church. She also signed me up for an after school program called "The Good News Club". It was where a handful of kids from school would gather to talk about God and Jesus and devise outlandish schemes that would spread the "good news" to each and every pair of ears deaf to the good Lord's call. It was here I met the notoriously thick-thighed whore and High School senior, Bessy Gustov. During my first meeting with the group, she sat next to me and smelled of roses and cucumber fairy dust. I knew about her reputation not mainly from the rumors polluting the hallways, but also because I caught Jimmy Shortrich in home room drawing an amateur illustration depicting him thrusting his blue-ink-colored dick between her thighs. He saw me staring and winked, pointing to the drawing down on the paper and mouthed silently, "oh yea." I just assumed she was a whore because thirty-seven other boys in the school had similar drawings stashed away in their lockers. I'm not sure what this meant because there was never any concrete confirmation of the deed being done. Bottom line: Bessy Gustov was sitting next to me. She chose to sit next to me. And through the pink, watermelon-flavored bubble gum in her chews she whispered to me: "Walk me home and I'll sit on your dick."

Three things happened after that: I lost my virginity to Bessy Gustov that evening, I never prayed to God again, and Jimmy Shortrich caught me scribbling a half-assed pen and ink of Bessy Gustov with her thighs wide the hell open for my lead-shaded cock to slide in. I got the thumbs up.

At the next "Good News Club" meeting, I imagined the polite thing to do would be to sit next to Bessy and maybe let her know that I still wanted to be friends. I'd heard that girls liked that sort of thing.

Disappointingly, she never showed. Thinking about it further, I couldn't remember seeing her at school at all that day. After the meeting, I took the after school bus home, but instead of my usual routine, I got off at her stop. Bessy lived a few blocks away from me, three stops before mine. So walking home from her place wasn't that big a deal. I figured I'd stop by and see if she was home. Not to be creepy or anything. Just to make sure she wasn't dead. I wasn't attracted to her that way, I didn't want to be her fucking boyfriend. But something compelled me to want to see her again. Something about the way she kissed and nibbled my ear lobe.

Bessy Gustov lived in one of those houses you rarely see in real life. The kind of place with the sides and the front painted dark and with the windows ominous and threatening. The grass in the front lawn was frequently overgrown, and there was never a car in the driveway. It was then I took note of the realization that Bessy took her wardrobe inspirations directly from her house. With hands in my pockets, I climbed the porch steps with creak after tickling creak. Closer inspection revealed a mailbox by the front door stuffed with armful after armful of envelopes.

From behind, a man wearing a stagnantly slutty pair of hiked-up navy blue shorts and a faded beige safari hat approached, carrying a tattered tote bag labeled "USPS".

"Afternoon," he said cheerily, brushing passed, "you're the first person I've seen here in a few weeks. If you're here to see the-" he looked down at the envelopes he was about to stuff into the mailbox, "Gustov's...I don't think you'll find much satisfaction." Interesting way to say that no one was home. He stood there for a moment, almost catching his elbow on the rusted swinging bench to his right. "Yea I don't know when exactly they left, but no one's been around here for a while. Here, have a rubber band! You have a good day, now." The man who seemed to think I was seven years old who still got a boner over postmen giving out rubber bands tipped his safari hat, hopped on down the porch steps and strolled on to the next house, whistling through his teeth and humming something through his lips that was probably supposed to sound self-motivating.

I peered in through the windows on either side of the front door. The glass was grey, and greased over with some kind of blackening paste. Almost as if someone couldn't get enough darkness from those fabled room-darkening shades you could get at Home and Garden Surplus. My mother had gotten them for my father when he started working night shift a few years ago. He said they "barely did shit, and would serve a better purpose had they been marketed towards sumo wrestlers who couldn't get enough bang for their buck while purchasing standard toilet paper."

From what little I could see, the dining room table appeared to have been set for three. Bessy and her parents. Plates were set out. Forks and knives. Napkins neatly folded atop the plates. Even a bottle of white wine accompanied by two wine glasses had been set out.

"I knew someone who drank white wine once," my mother once murmured and giggled, glass of red in her hands, "she was a fucking whore."

A gust of wind kicked up a swirling mist of dirt and sand around me. Some of the particles found their way into my nostrils, forcing a sneeze outta me. When my misty-eyes cleared, I found a pair of gleaming eyes peering back at me through the window. Bessy's eyes. She took my be surprise by before I could motion toward the door she fell from sight. I didn't hear from her after that. I didn't see her in school nor in the "Good News Club". Nothing. Not even a poke.

Three days later, I found myself sitting on our little double tweed couch in front of the television. We'd just eaten dinner and had sat down to enjoy our weekly Tuesday night viewing of this show called "The Catapult". I didn't like it. My father sure as shit didn't like it. But my mother said the relationships between the characters are what was important, that they always found a way to "catapult" themselves over their obstacles. Hence the name of the show. Fucking cute.

As the three of us gathered around the tube, and the fried salmon and chicken-flavored rice and garlic green beans settled in our bellies, the opening credits flicked on. My mother was knitting. My father was fighting back Z's. And I couldn't stop thinking about Bessy. I couldn't tell if it was fate or coincidence that our show was interrupted by a "Breaking Report" titled "Massacre in Swedestown, New Jersey".

"We would like to take this time to warn viewers of the nature of this report as to be disturbing and not for the faint of heart. Not long ago," Jenny Gardner, the hot blonde-tutored, infinitely-breasted anchor who was perpetually dressed like a Christmas Tree started, "authorities discovered the remains of Frederick and Genie Gustov in the basement of their home, after an anonymous call from a neighbor reported seeing their daughter leave the house with a large trash bag in the middle of the night. The neighbor reportedly went outside under the guise of walking their dog and inspected the trash bag to find the head of Mr. Gustov and what was later to be identified as the big toes of Mrs. Gustov. The rest of the remains of their bodies were discovered after said neighbor called the police. Bessy Gustov remains in custody at Swedestown County. More of this as it develops."

My mother stared blank-faced at the television screen, Kardashian-inspired eye liner tearing down her cheeks. My father sat next to me blinking heavily. The resumed opening credits of "The Catapult" scrolled across the television screen.

"Had to have been Trip Pickard. Bastard is

always nosing through someone's trash," my father muttered, "caught the guy sifting through Chuck's garbage the other night. Chuck said he had to chase him off with his son's bamboo bo staff thing from karate class. I swear the people in this town are just...peculiar."

The only thing I could think of saying was:

"I lost my virginity to a murderer."

Thirty years later, I found myself sitting in my new psychiatrist's waiting room along with six other multi-ethnical patients. The walls imprisoning us were papered a pale blue color that I read in Feng Shui Digest were supposed to "decrease hostiility, and increase a desire to be Christ-like." Personally, the color was so pale, I'd rather crucify my dick and present it to the Pope as evidence for stigmata.

"What are you in for?" the pimped-out Buick-shaped man sitting two seats over from me was reading a three-month old issue of Home Garden. I know the issue was three months old, because I browsed through it three months ago. There was an article inside on cactus care that interested me. I remember taking the test at the end of the article. Turns out I put recreational drug use before my yard's botanical needs.

"When I was fifteen years old, I lost my virginity to a murderer," usually I wasn't akin to telling strangers the truth about my presence, but today was different. Today, I was turning forty-five, and I there were one or two bones in my body that were sluts for tradition.

"Really?" the man's glasses seemed to fog up, but I think that was just my imagination.

"I never tell a lie," I smiled. The man swallowed,

stood up and approached the receptionist's desk, "would you please tell Dr. Flesko that Howard Bungalo would like to reschedule his appointment? I uh...I need to go." And with that, he hurried out of the office, sweating profusely and almost tripping over the edge of the carpet on his way out. I've been in therapy for thirty years. And for twenty-six of those years on my birthday, I've told an unsuspecting victim about my flavor of psychological damage. Their reactions were my own little birthday gifts to myself.

"I see things in windows and I say to myself that I want them. I want them because I want to belong. I want to be liked by more people, I want to be held in higher regard than others. I want to feel valued, so I say to myself to watch certain shows. I watch certain shows on the television so I can participate in dialogues and conversations and debates with people who want the same things I want. I want to dress a certain way so certain groups of people are forced to be attracted to me. I want to do my hair a certain way with certain styling products and particular combs and methods so that I can fit in with the In-Crowd. I want to spend hours upon hours at the gym, stuffing my body with what scientists are calling 'superfoods', so that I can be loved and envied by everyone around me. I want to become an icon on someone's mantle. I want to work meaningless jobs so that I can fill my wallet and parentally-advised bank accounts with monetary potential. I want to believe what's on the news so that I can feel normal along with the rest of forever. I want to listen to the Top Ten on Q102, and roll my windows down so others can hear it and see that I am listening to it, and enjoying it. I want to go to church every Sunday, and pray every other day. I want to believe that what I do is for the promise of a peaceful afterlife. I want rewards for my 'good' deeds. I want acknowledgment and praise. And I want people to know that I put out that fire. I want people to know that I support the war effort. I want people to know that I volunteer to save lives. I want to be seen and heard and pointed at with love. I want to read my name in the history books during a future full of clones exactly like me. The mirror, I've noticed, is almost always positioned above the sink. Though the sink offers more depth than a mirror, and mirror is only able to reflect, the sink is held in lower regard. Lower still is the toilet, and thought it offers even more depth than the sink, we piss and shit in it. I want these kind of architectural details to be paralleled in my every day life. I want to care more about my reflection, and less about my cleanliness. I want to be seen as someone who lives externally, and never internally, unless I am able to lock the door behind me. I want these things, because if I didn't, I would be dead in the mirrors of those around me. I would be nothing. I would be an example. Sunken, and easily washed away."

Doctor Flesko remained behind his desk, eyes fixated upon the thrity-two inch computer flatscreen. Through the reflection of his John Lennon-styled glasses, I could see that he was scrolling down his Facebook Fan Page again. "Doctor Flesko's Free Therapy", it was called. He'd once caught me catching him not listening to my verbalized woes and had explained to me its purpose as a consolation prize for my subsequent woe.

Generous prick.

"Yea, it's uh," the twenty-eight year old, fresh outta school manchild with fake pubes growing from his chin, cool-styled slicked back hair motherfucker had said, "it's for my patients who can't afford my services. Just got up to three-thousand likes today too, which is amazing considering I only have twelve in-office patients." Doctor Flesko was born out of wedlock by a very well-off couple living somewhere in the higher-end side of North Jersey. His parents had only gotten married because if they didn't their families would crucify their private parts all over their community that would shame their family names for generations to come. Because of this, Doctor Flesko was treated like a prince. Brought up in the finest schools. Given his own checking account at age ten. Given his own pick of the automotive litter at age sixteen so that by the time he turned seventeen and actually got his license, his car wouldn't be brand new and full of fuckups. Doctor Flesko graduated at the top of his class through careful negotiations mainly from his father's part. His mother wrote his University Application Letter and his father paid the Dean a hefty sum to ensure graduation was never an issue. I knew all of this because I've read Doctor Flesko's second biography, "Biography of a Regretful Rich Kid: The Life and Times of a Cursed Yuppie". I think it was his way of voicing his own acknowledgment of how easy he's had it and blaming his parents for never letting him fail in the same way most of us lucky ones have.

And now here I sat in his office. For the seventeenth appointment since the state aid notified me of my coverage changing, which included a whole new policy AND a new psychiatrist/ physician. I was never a huge fan of these sorts of changes, but I liked to occasionally pride myself with the ability to roll with the punches. That was until I came to meet this asshole: a kid glued to social media more than his own personal clients. Stacked neatly on the bookshelf behind his head, there were dozens of books shelved with the intention of making one believe that he actually read once in a while. The variable layers of dust populating the shelves and spines of titles like "Zen Pro", and "Aphrodisiacs for Addicts", and "She Comes First: A Study Two-Thousand Years in the Making", and "Bowling for Concubines" contradicted that theory.

"Doctor," I spoke up, words just above the clicking of his mouse as he scrolled down his Fan Page, "did you hear anything I just said?"

"Sure did, you creep you," he had a fairly whimsical sense of humor when it came to addressing us psychos, "you want a lot of things, don't you?"

Despite me being significantly older than him, even with a parent-paid college degree and doctorate, he could never find a way to talk to me in any way other than as if I were in First Grade.

"I mean what do you want me to say exactly," he saw that I was becoming impatient. "You seem very...dejected from the rest of society, and there really isn't anything I can say other than to face your past...which judging from your files given to me by your old psych junkie, is clearly something you still need to confront. It's been thirty years, give or take.

That's a long time to hold something in."

"Don't you have any...like...drugs? A prescription, say to...dull myself....until I'm ready to make that confrontation?"

He looked at me as I were begging for a green card. I didn't want anything more to do with this jerk, especially if he wasn't going to even try to help me. Hell, read me a haiku. Paint me a picture and ask me what I think it looks like. Blindfold me and stick my hand in the secretary's cooch for all I care. SOMETHING. All he did was shake his head and return to his thirty-two inch computer screen.

"Look," I sighed, "I know you're just a guy given to me by the damn state. I know you think I'm some piece of shit lazy asshole who can't get a job and sucks the life outta the world with his own welfare, but I'm really just...a guy. With problems. I'm sure you've got issues somewhere in there. Hell maybe enough to write a third book, I don't know. You're not married, maybe you want to get married. You need to open up too, hoss! Use that facebook bullshit! Talk to people! All I'm saying is I'm a person too." He licked his lips, blinking and stroking an invisible wall of contemplation. I had just explained to him the importance of compassion...but what I really wanted to do was slam that goddamned computer monitor overtop his head and call it a day.

"I'm going to write you a prescription," he started scribbling on a piece of yellow paper with his left hand, "now, pay attention. Because this is VERY important. You'll go to the pharmacy next door. The pharmacist is one of my colleagues. Give him this paper and he'll take you out back. Once out back, he'll give you the stuff. I don't do this for everyone, so consider yourself lucky." He handed me the paper, but as I reached out to grab it, he grabbed my hand as if to shake it, like men do, "the stuff he is going to give you is strong. Got it? Strong. You've never had it before. And if anyone asks, you've never had it before. Say nothing to anyone. Say nothing to anyone as you leave here. Don't even stop to check out my secretary's tits. Don't stop to pat the back of the security guard out front. Just....walk. Got it?"

As I left his office, and I stepped into the stone-cold apathetic embrace of the pale-blue-papered waiting room, I stepped by the secretary's desk and stopped for a moment. She had cleave that must have dug down to China.

"I see you looking at me again," she said. The tips of her brown curls did the laughing. "If you continue to stare I'll make sure your state aid is either revoked or suspended. Am I clear?"

"Virgin," I muttered and left. My cell phone vibrated at the exact moment the fresh Detroit Skyline air invaded my nostrils. Down on the screen I read I status update...

Doctor Flesko's Free Therapy: "Shutting down for a week or so guys. I've suddenly been made aware of a family emergency. Direct your questions and concerns to my private email and I will respond as soon as this hiatus is over."

A dirt, blood, and piss-stained Detroit Police Squad Car drove passed, flicking its sirens into the air, letting us mortals know of its presence. Walking the opposite direction, Homeless Heppy strolled passed drinking from a paper bag and cursing Bob Saget for raising him on false hopes. It began to snow, and with each fallen flake I found myself thirstier and thirstier for a bonfire.

I looked at the yellow piece of paper he'd given me. On it was written the following:

"This is Randall Winston Cunningham. He's one of my more...in-need patients. I'm sending him to you as a means to settle yours and my debt. Hopefully he can be of assistance and then we can just forget about the whole thing. Give him the stuff, and he'll do whatever you need. I'm sorry for everything, Ben, really. Just...I hope this counts as an apology. Love, Flesky."

All I could say was:

"Fuck, what the?"

I'm not what you might call a very intelligent individual. Occasionally I use words in my every day speech like "tender" or "morose", and sometimes to spice things up I throw in a little barnyard onomatopoeia. The essence of my mental distillery cannot be found in the words I choose to populate my voice, but rather the random split decision that if not elected could otherwise mean the end of my life. So with that said, I turned my flabby ass around and marched right back into that government-rented office building, pushed passed the security guard, winked at the Republican secretary and turned the knob entering Doctor Motherfuckin' Flesky's office.

I started off by throwing the little piece of yellow paper in his direction with the intent of it slapping him in that big Jewish nose of his. Being the tiny little slab of life that it was, the paper simply stopped midair and drifted disjointedly down to his desk like an autumn leaf.

"I am not some piece of almost homeless ass you can just pass off as fodder for whatever sex trade you're obviously financing, bub," I mean, given the circumstances and possibilities...wouldn't you?

His mouth opened, and the cracks of his mouth revealed what a veterinarian might recognize as rabies foam.

"I will not...I REFUSE to be treated that way, understand?! All I want is something to numb the brain with a little more strength than the everyday George Dickle. That shit gets expensive. Now for real, doc, gimmie something with soul!"

The level of foam rose with the personality of an apocalyptic wave from Noah's back yard, quickly blocking his entire mouth. Face turning red, like a goddamn tomato straight from mama's garden, he began to choke. His neck did this little half-assed Macarena thing. He coughed, eyes bulging like grapes....and then face-planted right onto the desk.

Authorities would later explain to me and everyone else in the office that Doctor Flesko died of an apparent overdose of something called "25C-NBOMe", a type of LSD. I left the office thinking..."well...that's alright then. One less asshole." Two hours later I made it home, having taken the long way and ignoring all forms of public transportation. Then again it was Detroit after all. An actual homeless man once told me, "Along any given path of life, it doesn't matter which way you take home. Ill intentioned-folk hold no sway over our karma." I only remember that because I never saw him again.

II. Inheritance

I lived in what was once a halfway housing building used as a shelter for the homeless. It'd never been upkept during those years, so everything, even the flower garden out front took on a very somber appearance. Pink was burgundy. Green was sludge. Blue was a heart attack. And black was just....blacker. The place was capable of housing seventeen families on each of its seventeen floors. But only during the colder months were they ever that populated. There were no tenants or Room Advisors, no guards, no receptionists, nothing that might otherwise lead one to believe it to be a legitimate apartment building. So if you had to use the laundry room on the third floor, your best bet was to spot the eight-year old illegal alien child two floors down a piece of Bazooka Joe so he'd let you use his hose out back. The most we had was variably-reliable electricity, and running water reaching temperatures not much colder than the last hooker I dated. I shared an apartment-sized unit with three other people. Women, of course. All of them under the age of thirty with IQ's not much higher than their shoe sizes. And every night I came home, they were up to something moronic. For instance, tonight:

"Hold still, I'm not ready," Michelle, the youngest and most scantily clad of the three, was filling the sink with water. In the kitchen were the other two, Dawn and Franny Wilcox, sisters by anything but blood. Dawn held a camera ready to film whatever it was Michelle was planning on doing while Franny had her left hand jammed down her pants, scratching her asshole as usual. "OK," Michelle started, adjusting her bra, "my name is Michelle Langrodose, and I've been nominated by my roommates Dawn and Franny Wilcox to do the Sink Head Challenge. I nominate my friend Jimmy Toobit, Chuck Powers, and my mother, Rhonda, wherever the fuck she is, to donate a hundred dollars to the Cure AIDS OR DIE Group, or to dunk their heads in a sink full of water."

"Water looks less brown than it did yesterday," I muttered to Franny, who giggled. Michelle dunked her head, surfaced, and immediately began laughing her whore ass off.

"How'd therapy go," Dawn asked. I grabbed a beer from the fridge but Franny snatched it from me, stuffing the cap end up her cooter. "Oh watch this, this is great!" Dawn bit her lower lip in anticipatory glee while Franny twisted the bottle of brew half-jammed up her cunt. There arose a crack and a whisper...a queef with panache. Two seconds later, Franny handed me back my beer, bottle cap removed. She winced a little, and then out popped the cap, bouncing atop the kitchen floor tile beneath her.

"If you don't want to drink that, I won't be offended," Franny said. Franny, by all dictionarial right...was a real life hooker, much like my ex. Except my ex was proven to be clean in the poon, and always made time to go to the clinic no matter what sort of demands her pimp made. Franny on the other hand...let's just say I'd rather be sentenced without parole life in a sauna that smelled like granny diaper shit than let my beloved smelling abilities have anything to do with whatever lived between her legs. And so I handed her the beer and grabbed myself a fresh one.

"Therapy was....well, the doc killed himself," I lit a cig, pursing it between my lips and taking a stroll on over to the jizz and cat-piss-stained couch. "I don't think I'm missing much anyway." Looking down at my phone, I checked his Facebook Fan Page. Already there were hundreds upon hundreds of posts running down the wall like tears, from hundreds upon hundreds of people pretending to know the bastard, thanking him for whatever advice he'd given them. I imagined what it would be like when I died. I imagined my childhood coming to a sudden close, and all matter of things whispering its last and final whisper. And then I imagined it wouldn't really matter when I died. I'm living with three women in a building that's ready to fall over with the slightest increase of wind speed. Most of the buildings in this town were like that anyway. Only benefit of living in this one was we were allowed to light bonfires in the hallways.

"You look sad," Dawn plopped her cottage cheese thighs down beside, her cleavage an astounding "yes" to my subconscious "no". She'd spent nearly her entire time since moving in with me, trying to give me a reason to let her suck my cock. Or fuck my cock. Dawn was a self-proclaimed damaged sort of lass with an infinite compendium of childhood rape stories. I didn't exactly have a reason to not believe any one of them, but something in my bones told me that maybe she was just looking for attention. A reason to be loved. "Anything I can do for ya?" She started every attempt in this fashion, running her fingertips along my shoulders, eventually journeying down my belly and across my chest. I admit, I only allowed the contact to last as long as it did because it felt good. To be touched by a woman. I didn't want anything to do with her soul, or God forbid, her vagina, but her fingertips were okay in my book. They reminded me of what it felt like to cry in private. A release that no one on this earth deserved to witness. Her lust was the fuel to my impersonal meditation. If I could put my feelings down in writing, they'd say something along the lines of: "And then she kissed me."

But we all know such tragedies only exist in soundless dreamscapes. And even if I let her kiss me, I'd be doing nothing more than giving her a false hope. And I wasn't in any way, shape, or fucking form, a man of false hopes.

"I'm tired," was my usual response. "get any cash today?"

"If I say 'no', it means that I'm lying," she laughed, "but if I say 'yes', it means that I only did it because we needed it, and not because they meant anything to me. I want you to know that."

"I don't care who the fuck you fuck," I coughed and hacked, guzzling the rest of my beer, "desperate times call for-"

"Yea well fuck you too," Dawn slapped the bottle from my lips, sending it across the room and crashing against the nearest wall, barely inches from where the last one hit. I grabbed her wrist, pulled her back down to the couch before she could get up.

"I was drinking that, you smut," pushing her away, she cracked her head on the coffee table, not far from the edge she hit last time. She scrambled to her feet, and wiped away the blood from her lower lip.

"You're a piece of shit, Winst."

"Moo," nailed it, "Look bitch, no one is forcing you to stay, hell I never asked you to come in! So FUCK YOU and your diseased fucking self! You can stay if you want, but I will never, EVER stick myself between your legs. Get that shit through your HEAD, YOU THING!" She hated when I called her a thing. She once said that it reminded her of her father. But I had to get the message through to her somehow. I had to slam the door home...had to make her aware of just how serious I was. And she never left. Ever. Every fresh batch of bruises were just a reminder to her that she'd be subject to worse should she leave.

And every night when I found myself alone, when Dawn and the others piled into their holes and tucked themselves in, or passed out on the kitchen floor, or tempted fate with a new syringe....I found myself alone. We used to have a fully functional mirror in the bathroom, along with a fully functional toilet. But like everything else flowing though our veins on the way to our heart, it ran its course long ago.

I flushed the toilet.

It was 3:12 a.m. That meant that there wasn't a sound to be heard other than the other toilets flushing in the building. The pipes liked to pretend they were a Cincinnati Orchestra like that. Occasionally, when at last the building neighborhood mothers put their little welfare shits to sleep, and all the drunks and dust-sniffers had their fill, deep blasts of wind could be heard howling through the halls through each of the grease-stained, shit-smeared windows.

Corridors like the throats of old men, coughing and hacking their lungs to the beat of incessant rainfall and crying and fucking. Patter patter patter....cough cough cough....hack hack hack....the building was one big old man...breaking at the ankles, collapsing at the knees...just ready for a single, massive, foundation-shattering heart attack to bring it all and all of its inhabitants down to their deaths. Wind through these halls, was just that old man's attempt to breathe.

It was 3:12 p.m.

I was sitting in my mother's lawyer's office somewhere on the upper end of Bernard Street, as if that alone could justify anyone feeling safe. I'd been called in because...well, the bitch finally kicked the bucket. The bitch being my mother. Let's just go with that. Apparently, she had this thing called a Will, and evidently she'd included me in it. Good to know her memory hadn't been completely shot.

Before me sat the man. The lawyer. Someone named Julius H. Dean. I imagined the H stood for something like Howard, or Harold. Something that made the coins in his purse jingle a little louder. His hair slicked back like a whale's tail, shining under the pale office ceiling lamp like a beacon of some kind. He wore a suit like a champ, I'll give him that. Part of me wanted to know where he got it so I could pick up one myself. For my coffin, that is. I wouldn't be caught anything but dead wearing whatever brand he was wearing.

"So, Mr....Cunningham," Dean's voice reminded me the sound a jelly jar makes when a kid scrapes the bottom with a knife for that last little bit; the headache maker, "your mother, as you know, died several days ago." to add insult to fuckery, his tone sat as dry as stale toast. Probably the same toast that kid was hoping to spread his jelly over.

"Something about a suicide," I said, remembering Dean's voice over the phone when he called, "fucking epidemic."

"Yea well," he sighed, "she had something sent here that in her Will specifically states to play for you upon the moment of her demise. Strange because it's a video...but it was sent to my email almost seconds after her death. Almost like she'd planned it all along."

"Isn't that what suicide is? A plan?"

"Sure it is," Lawyer Man shrugged, "well...uhm....I guess I should go ahead and hit play." He had it already loaded on the computer screen for me. All he had to do was hit play. The video started playing, and at once there appeared a title slide, opening credits one might say.

"Goodbye, My Son," the main title said, "A Tribute to a Life I Never Wanted," read the subtitles, "Directed by Samantha Beverly Waterloo," she'd changed back to her maiden name after divorcing my father some years ago. The video opened, and there she sat in all her overweight glory. Fat Mamma. Giant jowls. Bright blonde curly hair. And a smile not even a school kid could love. But there she was. Sitting in her room at her desk. The first thing I noticed was the noose hanging from the ceiling fan dangling a few feet behind her.

"Hello, Randall!" She smiled, and I felt as if this were some sort of webcam date, "My dear boy, I know it's been forever, and rightly so. You being a little bastard and abandoning me and all. But I say let's let the past be the past for once. I wasn't exactly the best mother a kid could have, obviously. And if you're watching this and you're smart enough to notice that old rope in the background, you know what's about to happen," I couldn't get over how pleasant she sounded; she smiled like my dog Zepp used to when I'd returned home from school every day, "I've been...well, I've been contemplating lately about all those years ago when I probably should have done certain things differently, particularly when it came to raising you. I think the real fortune cookie realization started around the time I caught you....well," she made a motion down by her crotch, like a boy does when he's looking at Home and Garden Magazine because his older brother stole and stashed away all the Hustlers. Julius H. Dean's eyebrow arched so hard it stabbed me in the left ear, "I think your father used to call it, um, churning dairy or something. Oh I don't know. I suppose it's not that important. Anyway, I think it was at that moment I started down a dark path. The one all parents fear," in the background, a sunrise-white cat appeared as if from nowhere, and took it upon itself to stalk the hanging noose. Staring up at it, the cat made several swat attempts, regardless of how high up and out of reach it was, "I love you son, but I-" the cat leapt up suddenly, grabbing hold of the loop of the noose and swang left and right. My mother caught this and rectified the situation the same way she fixed everything. "Oh damnit! Madonna! Get off that thing! Madonna! Damnit! Come here!" She grabbed the cat by its tail and tossed it across the room. "That's not for you!" She vanished from sight for a moment, and a door could be her shutting. Seconds later, she sat back down in front of the camera, and adjusted her smile. "Sorry, damn cats make everything worse sometimes," she giggled, "okay, so. Bottom line...I fucked up, son. I messed up bad. My doc says I've got perfect health so...it'll probably be a long time if I wait for natural causes to take me. The only way I can ever make anything up to you is by doing this, and leaving my house and all of my belongings to you. You deserve it son. So. With that said, it's time to pass on the torch," she backed away from the camera, placed a stool on top of her bed, just below the noose, climbed aboard, and slipped her head through the loop. "I love you son, this one is for you!" But before she could take any sort of heartfelt leap, the stool twisted and contorted. It's rebellion against gravity came to a close. My mother fell awkwardly, and her weight alone caused the ceiling fan to lose its grip on life. The ceiling fan buckled, but didn't fall. Instead, the noose snapped, and the fat, chunky, jiggly whale of a carcass that was my mother bounced off the bed and fell to the floor with a thud.

Above her, the fan hung by a thread.

"Jesus H. Christ," Dean gasped.

My mother started climbing to her feet, tossing out swears and obscenities like old chewed up gum. The ceiling fan swung a little from the recent breach of indenture, and suddenly fell...giving out entirely. Before my mother could spit out another "damnit", the fan struck her head, like a sea otter cracking a shellfish over a rock...and she was gone.

End video. Fade to black. Email sent.

"What the hell was that?" Was all I could

muster.

"Well," Dean scratched his elbow, "not all suicides are the same."

"No I mean...what the HELL was that?! How did you get the video?"

"She must have had it sent automatically. People are doing wonders with computers these days. You know there's a site where you get type in any sort of key combination, and the output will activate a paid-escort's toy of choice in any way you want? Amazing. I don't know why I used that example, but it's definitely something to think about."

"So then," I started, "she's dead. And I get her house?"

"And everything in it, which is quite a lot. You'll have to travel though. Let's see, uh...her house is in...Tonas, Pennsylvania. Just south of Philadelphia."

"So basically, trash. Great."

"She's got a pool, and so most of the neighbors! That's a lot of pool party barbecues and such! Your mother really loved those."

"I don't give a goddamn shit about no goddamn barbecue or a goddamn pool. I'm not a genius, but I know all of this is still gonna cost me. Upkeep. You know?"

"So get a job. Your mother always used to complain about how resentful she was to explain to relatives how long you've been unemployed. Get a job. Something. Anything. There's enough money in her accounts to hold you over for a while, but everything runs out eventually. It's time to grow up, Mr. Cunningham."

"So by growing up...you mean for me to get a

job? You mean, get up every morning at 4 a.m. and ride a bus full of potential rapists to a place where I'll not only work my fat ass off for next to zero pay, but also be completely and morosefully unappreciated for all my hard work? Only just to retire thirty...well maybe twenty-five, years later for a pension I could make my sucking a few cocks a week in the richer part of town? Get a job. Sorry, I'm worth more than that."

Mr. Dean shot me a look that spoke several expletive variances on how I was the only one who believed that. He then asked if I was assigned a new therapist yet.

Mr. Dean told me he'd contact me tomorrow with more info regarding paperwork and all that bullshit. I returned to my home with the hookers and found Michelle sitting up on the kitchen counter like a smeagol, shooting up what was probably the last of her supply. I could hear the muffled moans of Franny from somewhere in the apartment, which probably meant she was working. And Dawn was standing out on the balcony, overlooking a future that would always be hers.

"I inherited a house today," I said, stepping out onto the ledge beside her, "it's around Philly. Furthermore it's away from here."

"Congrats," she sucked in her nicotine, lips quivering, waiting for me to tell her that I was going alone.

"I wanted to know if you would go with me."

And that right there, would eventually become known to myself, and those closest to me, as the worst decision ever made and would ever make.

Children populated the city's educational

institutions in the exactly the same fashion the paper factories polluted the atmosphere. The irony being we all breathed the same air. And that particular Monday morning, thick into the middle of July's vagina, it snowed just as it had yesterday. And with each frustration-scented snowflake that fell, with each idiotic, parentless kid running passed us, with each breath of Detroit air Dawn and I sucked in-

"So your mother...AND your therapist commit suicide at about the same time? What is that some sort of joke?" Dawn asked, interrupting my thoughts. She and I had offered Michelle and Franny each a ticket on board our flight; the two of them declined as expected, each of them glued to their work. Couldn't blame them. Free sex all the time, all day, all night. They didn't care what sort of dicks slipped between their legs. As long as they got a cut of the fee. As long as it put food on their plates. As long as it was only illegal and not frowned upon in this sort of town.

Before Dawn and I stood on the sidewalk, I'd found her thrown over her bed face down, arms dangling over the edge as if she'd been reaching for something and had fallen asleep in the process. The room reeked of piss, but that wasn't anything out of the ordinary; the room and the hallway always smelled like piss. Michelle and Franny had been home the night I first noticed it, but neither of them gave up the truth of the cause. So when I say the room smelled like piss, I mean that just as it was. You never really get used to the smell...sometimes it fades, sometimes it lingers, but it never truly dissipates.

Her head hung over the far side of the bed, a dried pile of yellow vomit clung to the carpet just beneath her face; tips of her unwashed hair tiptoed upon the pile's surface. Still clinging in her left hand was an empty bottle of something too strong to do the math. I kicked her feet, still clad in her leather boots. Upon zero reaction, I kicked again, harder. She stuttered, spat a chunk of pukage that hadn't made it all the way out of her mouth, and looked at me with blood-red eyes.

She asked if it was time to go already. I told her to shine on you crazy fucking diamond. Helped her to her feet. And threw her coat in her face. Told her it was cold outside. She said it was always cold outside. And now here we stood. Waiting for a cab to take us to the airport.

Dawn and I each packed one carry-on. In our line of work, an unemployed, undiagnosed psychology-major's wet dream and a toe-jam fancied hooker with next to zero religion besides the Jew in her wallet didn't require much to get by. Without explaining too deeply into it, the bitch and I had a history, which was part of why I asked her to come along with me. Part of me would feel strange if she wasn't at least in the next room. Most of the time, wherever we went, and Detroit wasn't the only place we'd lived together, we would pool together our belongings as behave as a married couple from hell.

"If you've ever blindly face-planted into a window or glass sliding door, you already have one of the key fundamental ingredients needed to get through life. Question is, if someone had told you the door was closed, would you have still tried to walk through the glass anyway?" This was Dawn's and my philosophy, as written on the back of a coke bottle we found during one of their "Wisdom" Themed Promotions. It seemed to ring a little true with us, at least more true than the other bullshit bottles we picked up. When we finally found our seats on the plane, in the little magazine holder on the back of the seat in front of me, I picked out a little paperback book and started reading, hoping that its title "Menagerie Man" wasn't too misleading. I didn't read the back. But I did see the author's picture there. Asian man. Looked to be in his sixties. Named Grant Smith. Funny name for someone so...Asian looking. Dawn muttered that she never took me for the reading type. I told her to order some drinks so she could drunk herself to sleep so I wouldn't have to deal with her usual bullshit.

"It was summertime," the first page began, "and ninety degrees in every direction. I was 17 years old. I didn't have a job. And so I didn't really care about anything. This year was special because I was supposed to get my driver's license sometime in the next few weeks, but when everyone I've ever known was always behind the wheel anyway, why rush learning the difference between the gas and the brake just yet?"

Dawn must have been reading along with me, because I caught a look from her that must have been illustrating a string of politically-incorrect judgments. I shrugged, pushing her face away, and told her to look out the window, that I'd given her the window seat for a fucking reason.

"You can tell you're between a rock and a hard place when you're sitting on a rock, looking up at the night sky," an hour later, the bottom of the page read, "Or stumbling out of a stranger's house at 7 a.m. after a night of worshiping immortality, and being smacked in the face with a bright, bright sun; refreshing and Utopian all the same."

I didn't have to worry about Dawn's judgments this time around. Earlier during the flight she told me she spotted a prospective fifty bucks two rows back. And so now she was in the bathroom thumping away while the flight attendants handed out more of those delicious peanuts.

"I mean, the world was once flat....isn't that proof enough that people can change?" Before the plane touched down, I slipped the book into my bag. I couldn't really tell you why, or what the book was even about. So far, all I'd gotten out of it was some guy had discovered a way to travel backward through time by listening to certain songs that reminded him of a discernible point in his past. The problem was, he wanted to travel into the future, because he didn't feel like he was going anyway in his present time, and the past was too painful to keep experiencing over and over again. I felt like I should at least try to finish it. So in the bag it went.

Dawn told me her "bathroom buddy" not only gave her his number, but tipped her an extra fifty because her "lips wrapped around his cock tighter and more succulent than his wife's ever could". I snatched the fifty out of her hand.

"First month's rent," I said, smiling.

Philadelphia International Airport was a shithole. And that goes triple for its "employees". Nine outta twelve of these suckers look like they'd been hired straight from the meal lines. No background checks. No credit history checks. Not that that bothered me exactly...it meant that if my skin was painted a shade of a more molasses-persuasion, I could land a job here no problem.

The first difference I noticed severing Detroit from Philly was the weather. No snow here yet. Only sunlight. Smog, yes, but definitive sunlight. Dawn and I looked like a couple of retards in our coats. But that's okay. In any sane man's medical log book, we probably were retards. But at least we had coats. And so, we stood under the turquoise sky, our bags in hand, and hailed a cab. Told the Muslim motherfucker to take us to Tonas, the resting place of my dear suicidal mother, her mansion, and all of her belongings.

III. Astrea

The whole drive, Dawn was trying to apply what she liked to call "cosmetics of a distinguished hooker maiden". I told her she'd look hideous no matter what she did to her face, because it was fucking true. Our Muslim driver didn't like that. He said I should respect women, to do otherwise was impolite. I told him to fuck off, that he's the last fucking asshole who should give advice about respecting women when he probably makes his wife wear one of those identity-stealing hoods. I called that asshole a fucking hypocrite. And he went ballistic, saying something to me in his native tongue that I obviously couldn't translate for shit. Dawn just laughed. To her, his words probably sounded like toilet bowl water when shit plopped into it.

The road home had a tiresome amount of bumps to it. Roadwork was obviously something the state swept under the carpet in this corner of the world. And if you were too slow to catch every pothole, the shining sun reflected off the hundreds of hubcaps strewn about the sides of the road like mile-markers. I imagined if I could find a scrapper in the area, or someone of similar occupational strides, I could make a fortune, and maybe Dawn wouldn't have to suck as many cocks just for a full plate of dinner each night. Of course, with the money my mother just gave me, I'm pretty sure if I wanted, neither the bitch riding next to me or myself would have to find a job before long.

Wrestling with the urge to tip the taxi driver or not, I ended up slipping him a piece of paper with Dawn's number scrolled on it. I told him if he got tired of his wife's hood gettin' in the way of a nice blow j, to call this number and the woman answering would make his Carpet-riding cock feel right at home. Strangely, he wasn't offended, and thanked me, telling me that he understands I must have my trials and hard times to go through in my own personal life, but I'll never know the true pain of what he as a Muslim has gone through. I patted him on the back and wished him well as he drove off.

I've seen houses like mom's before. Most of the time they exist only the front pages of websites selling home insurance or home security devices. These kinds of houses were perfect in their architecture from the ground up. Brick walls. White marble columns on either side of the front door(s). A mailbox that looked like it was painted gold but was actually solid fucking gold. A stone pathway leading from the street up through an endless, professionally maintained front lawn. I wasn't much for these sorts of places. Lord knew I hated the idea of pearly fucking gates welcoming me into the afterlife...but hell, if mum was giving me something like this without any payment other than her death, well...shit. I'll take it.

Part of me had been sad to leave my Detroit digs. I'd sort of always felt comfortable in dimly lit, run down places. Friends in high school and I used to party in places like that. It was just...comforting in a way. The way the fire burned inside, reflecting off the walls and ceiling and architectural patchwork. Places like that even had a certain smell...of age...of wisdom that you couldn't get in any of these new places. And why should new places be like that?

They're new. Inexperienced. Grappling with their youth and rejecting the triumphant education the past could give. Age; it is truly a dying breed.

There was no one to welcome us into this larger-than-life abode. Evidently mum didn't have a maid or a butler or even so much as a house nigger. I was impressed. Either she had too much pride, or she fired the fucker before taping that lousy excuse of a suicide video. And so Dawn the Hooker and I just, walked in. I turned the lock with the key Mr. Dean passed on to me, and in the door swept.

Upon immediate inspection and first impressions, Dawn said it reminded her of the house she'd been raised in. Dawn was not a particularly smart woman, much in the same way I was not exactly a genius, but she had a philosophical side that included a mantra painting a rather questionable psychological portrait of the difference between the places we are raised and the places where we grow up. I like to think that her brand of wisdom was something akin to that of a toy found at the bottom of a cereal box. A nice surprise. Useful for an indeterminable amount of time. Something your parents congratulate you for having stumbled upon. And then one day it goes missing. And you never see it again. The people who raised me never bought the kind of cereal with that sort of innocence at the bottom of the box; so whenever Dawn voiced herself, part of me felt like I was gaining back a bit of missed childhood, whether I agreed with her or not.

The place had a smell that reminded me of my childhood. But nothing like cookies or brownies in the oven. it smelled like those little rubber floatie devices you slip on your arms when your a kid so you won't drown. I used them for a while after every other kid in the pool ditched them because I wasn't ever very good at the swimming thing. It smelled safe. Mandated. Preserved. Artificial.

We were hungry. Because we weren't used to having a depth-less abyss for pocket cash, Dawn and I didn't stop anywhere from the airport on the way to here for food. So the first thing we did was raid the kitchen. I found a note taped to one of the cabinets reading: "Randall, I figured by now you must be some kind of alcoholic, so before I put the rope around my neck, I stocked the cabinet full of booze. An assortment if you will. I know I shouldn't exactly support your addiction, if it is in fact something you have, but I have just passed...so you will undoubtedly need something to help you cope. Happy trails, son. Love, mom."

Dawn laughed. She said I had a hell of a mother, and that part of her wished she could have met her. I informed her that up until the moment she discovered I had the ability to masturbate, she was a halfway decent gal. Speaking of halfway decent gals, from the window above the kitchen sink I was given a view of the neighbor's pad to the direct rear of my mother's There was a pool, aqua colored waters, and one of those semi-large palm trees that lit up to the beat of whatever tunes were playing through the backyard speaker system. You know the kind of speakers built precariously into the souls of fake rocks planted all around the yard and pool. And it just so happened these neighbors, whoever they were, included a daughter.

Sure, she'd been born with amber locks but she didn't deserve them, not yet anyway. You could tell this truth simply by the way her legs crossed, her toes dipping big toe first into the water and the correlation between that and her inability to tan. Her pale northeastern skin, made paler by her ignorance. I admired that most about her. I wouldn't even have to say hi to her. I wouldn't have to get to know her. I wouldn't have to ask her silly questions like...what's your fucking zodiac? I saw her, and I saw the promise of something that had yet to reach its beginning. She was untouched. Unfiltered. Undefiled. She was also very, very young. The sort of young someone like myself should never have anything to do with. Not even to ask to babysit. The girl was probably somewhere between 9th and 10th grade...the kosher years. At least those were the kosher years while I was in high school. This new generation's lexicon for their year's pet names wasn't altogether anything henceforth-worthy.

"She almost looks good enough to fuck," Dawn interrupted my thoughts, lighting a cig, "if she wasn't about fourteen and a quarter. I bet she dresses like a slut scarecrow during Halloween. Straw comin' outta her cooter and everything." I grabbed the nearest bottle of whatever alcoholic bliss was in shortest arm's reach and shoved it into my sidekick's face.

"Have ya ever tried french kissing a bottle of wine while drinking from it?" The bottle was a screw top, and very easy to open while seamlessly aiming to pour all over her face. "It's like drowning and loving it."

"Ah, I see you're already scoutin' out the neighbors," a familiar voice shot from the rear, and I looked. Dawn looked, and scowled. I'd already told her about Mr. Dean, my mother's lawyer. About his client-paid for suits. His slicked back hair with the special biotin-protein treatment. The way his loafers never seemed to slip on any and all surfaces. Judging from her opening expression, she wasn't at all prepared for how wrong her superficial assumptions had been, and how liberal she had been with her negativity. "Yea that there," he said, taking note that I'd been checking out the girl next door, "is Astrea Foster. Adopted daughter of Mark and Pamela Foster. Fifteen years old, straight B student, and likes swimming the most out of all the sports young kids have to choose from. I figure it's probably got something to do with how much time she spends out by the pool." He looked a bit disoriented when he saw that Dawn and I had begun to visually but silently wonder how he knew all this, "sorry. Creeper status. Creepy lawyer is also a stalker of small children, amiright? Wrong. I'm no rapist, even though my first wife had a thing for the....fantasy. Just don't go telling her that to her face, or any one of her feminist bimbo friends. Fun fact: a guy saying that every woman has a rape fantasy is about as socially offensive as a white guy referring to his homies as niggas. It's just not socially acceptable. Don't do it, trust me. The pain is not worth the strain. Hypocrisy is all about the flavor of the day at the ice cream stand of life. When and where. My second wife taught me that, before I caught her in bed with my lawyer. Surprised? Yes, well...even lawyers need support every now and again. ANYWAY, one of your mother's most favorable hobbies was bird watching. I suppose little Astrea over there became an involuntary ocular subject of hers now and again. But, anyhow, why I'm here is probably your chief concern, obviously. It's my fault really, I was still kind of in shock over your mother's suicide video...which I'm not even sure technically counts as a suicide....maybe self-manslaughter, but I doubt that'd hold up in court. But you never know these days, lawyers, with the right amount of financial backing, I'm sure, can spin pretty much anything."

"Jesus fucking Christ. You talk faster than virgin cums," Dawn spat. Dean only laughed, half-bowed, and motioned for me to pour him a glass of the boozies in my hand.

"As a lawyer, particularly Randy's mother's," he patted me on the back with the same condescending intensity a t-ball coach encourages his star hitter, "I have to not only be quick on my feet, but in the mouth as well. Learned a few tough lessons the hard way. Anyway," he pulled out a sheet of wrinkled up parchment, which looked to have been written years ago, "don't let the paper quality fool you," Dean seemed to share my curiosity, "your mother was one weird lady. Sometimes she liked to role-play with herself. Like, pretending she was a princess locked in a tower or something. That included writing 'rescue me' letters and sending them to knights that never existed. This here paper is what she used to... authenticate the experience. My guess is she ran out of plain white 8 by 12's and found this to be the best she could do. It's basically a list of prerequisites."

"For what exactly," I drank deep.

"Well," Dean chuckled, "you know your mother. While we were working up her Will, she had me file this right there at the end. Saying that you were not applicable to receive any of her Will-installed goodies if you fail to abide by her list of requests."

"Oh for the love of fucking God," Dawn grabbed the bottle from me, stuffed it down her throat, and drained it of all its contents.

"The paper reads: My dear son Randall should only be able to live in my to-be passed on homestead provided he abide by my following conditions: 1. He attends church every Sunday. 2. He eats only healthy food, and will provide a receipt at the end of each week to a Mr. Julius H. Dean, proving he has purchased food from any of the half-dozen health food grocery stores in the area. He will only need to provide receipts for three-months time. 3. Treat the neighbors with respect and be courteous of their right to privacy. And lastly, 4. That he attends my funeral," Dean snickered, turning the paper over to make sure there was nothing else on the other side. "Wow, what a woman."

"What a complete bitch," Dawn muttered in her usual fashion.

"A smart bitch," Dean pointed out, "alright then. That concludes my business here. I shall be around sometime tomorrow to check on the status of the house. That was also in the Will. That I...swing by...every now and then, on days or during times of my own discretion. Not to be a dick," more grinning, "most of the time I'll probably just raid the liquor cabinet. It's tough out there for a lawyer." He nodded in a very Julius H. Dean way. Stern-faced, cocky-curled lips. Self-aware of how silly he looked in his suit. He knew he only wore it for appearances, and he knew we knew that. I had a feeling we wouldn't be getting much trouble from this guy. But when he stepped out the front door, he looked back in just as I was shutting the door and called out: "Don't go having any orgies now, you silly hooker you." I assumed he was talking to Dawn.

"Fucker is creepy," she said.

"He won't be a problem," I said, cracking open a new bottle of vodka. Whiskey was my main drink of choice, but the moment called for something Russian.

I went to my mother's funeral, as per request. It was nothing special. There was the casket. The flower setups. The fake family smiles. I got a few handshakes from some cousins I haven't seen since I was twelve. But mostly what I got were stares and glances ranging from slight to moderate to hamstring-cutting intensity. A politically correct individual running for Mayor might say I was the black sheep of the Cunningham Clan. Dawn would say otherwise. She didn't go because funerals "made her feel uneasy". Coming from a professional hooker, all I could do was give her respect for being so deep.

I met this women who said she wasn't related to me in any way shape or form. There must have been a language barrier in place because all I remember is a pretty face with a pair of heavily-made up eyes coupled with a sensuous smile. She said something about how funerals always made her feel emotional; wet even. She went on to state her vagina's claim to fame was directly related to this. And of course, I was obligated to ask her to prove this heinous ridiculation. When she asked me what had drawn me to her and how it was I knew that she was hot for cock, I simply told her: "I've got what you might call a, magnetic personality. It's like a metal detector for clits and moist labias." She nodded, and then swallowed my dick like that last piece of dark meat at the dinner table on Thanksgiving.

After the eulogy, I skipped the burial ceremony because that wasn't explicitly part of the deal in mother's Will. Who wants to watch a casket being lowered into the ground anyway?

Good old Mr. Dean showed up though, just to make an appearance so as to ensure I was living up to my part of the deal. He wore those bullshit sunglasses that get darker the brighter the sun is. And since it wasn't all that bright out, it only looked as though there was a thin later of fog over his eyes. Very misleading. He shook my hand, made some comment about his first wife being a "whore-ish fuckshit", and then left.

By the time I got home...well, mother's house, as after that list snafu, it was sort of hard to think of it as MY house yet, the sun was still out. Warmth was my prophylactic, and Astrea the fifteen year old girl was hanging out by her pool again. I decided it was time to make my introduction.

The girl sat at the edge of the water, legs dangling into the pool's coolness. Her skin was pale as it had been yesterday, but up close it just seemed so...tasteful. Delicious to the eyes. I'm surprised to this day I hadn't been drooling. She seemed to take note of the suit I was wearing, which to be honest wasn't really much of a suit. Dark jeans with a slight tear in one knee, and a black sports jacket I bummed off someone from the old apartment building in Detroit. It still kind of smelled like old seafood and butt-fungus, but at funerals and other such family gatherings, appearances are everything. Astrea wore one of those red bikini's with the white polka dots. It fit perfectly around her lady-bits; practically begging to be torn off by the teeth of whoever was gawking. She had my attention, obviously. But I knew the rules. The laws rather. She was fifteen. I was...much...much older. So old I could be her retarded step-cousin thrice removed. And even IF there wasn't the whole age-dilemma, for someone like me to fuck someone so beautiful would not only be a reason for imprisonment, but also a crime against nature.

"You're standing in front of the sun," were her first words as she looked at me through her sunglasses. They were the over-larged type. The bug-eye specs that seemed to have a purpose meant more for shielding the entire face than just the eyes. "Sorry if that sounded rude. My dermatologist says I need more vitamin D in my skin diet. Says the pills are just bullshit. I need real, hardcore, quality actual sunlight." I moved to the side, and suddenly she was lit up like a candle again. "I'm Astrea," she held out her hand. I wanted to shake it, as polite peeps do, but I still hadn't taken a shower since moving in yesterday. And before that, I can't remember when I'd taken a shower at all...

"I'm Randall...Randall Cunningham," not exactly the James Bond of introductions, but as they say: at the buffet, there's something for everyone, "I uh...well I sure as shit didn't pay for this." Not sure why that was where I went first. I suppose it had something to do with the way whatever sunscreen Astrea was using glistened in her budding, pubescent cleavage. Wonders of the world and all.

"Uh...nevermind."

"It's nice to meet you, Randall. Randall Cunningham," she smiled. At least she got my name right. Score. Silence is very rarely ever warranted, but when it is, it's beautiful. Like stepping out beneath the moonlight sometime in early September, when Fall is just about to hit and the last fleeting remains of summer's dementia-soaked heat begin to dissipate. Or when snow falls. Silence always comes hand in hand in falling snow. A quiet sort of roar that only arises after the children have up and gone to bed. This was not one of those silences. Broken records have a more fruitful tone than this.

"I have a list," I said, trying to compensate; failing, "my mother's lawyer says if I don't abide by it I don't get the house," and then I laughed as if that last sentence was the punch line to a joke no one's ever heard. Clearly I wasn't ready for the dating scene. I did notice she had in her possession the latest model of whatever smartphone was most popular. She had earbuds plugged in and was fumbling with them in her fingers. "Fan of music I see."

"Yea. Isn't everybody?"

"Well," I shrugged, "one can hope."

"My father grew up pissing on The Beatles but preaching Lennon. It's about the only thing he and I see eye to eye on," she flashed me the screen on her phone. An album cover of one of John Lennon's musical tomes blinked. A door to the house opened before I had a moment to process what she'd said. A man walked out with a stiff stride and an expression that strayed. Despite the warmth of the

Pennsylvanian sun, he sported a red-flannel bust and snug-worn carpenter jeans. The man had a mustache. Not a pornstache, though, sadly. More like just a stachestache. Generic. Trimmed. like a black-haired caterpillar had been crawling across his face and died once it reached the space between his nose and his lips. Dead and stuck by some weird insect voodoo. "Speaking of my father," Astrea looked back as he stepped out into the sun.

"Daughter," he started, keeping his eyes locked on mine. His nose twitched in a way a deer does when it catches a whiff of something it doesn't like, "who is this man?"

"Oh, he's our new neighbor, he just moved in," Astrea smiled. "Randall Cunningham, this is my dad. Dad, Randall." I did what men do in movies and at church and held out my hand. He didn't seem like a man who liked contact much, but I figured I'd give him the benefit of a doubt for being at least a little bit polite.

"Mark," he said, still not holding out a hand, "spelled with a 'C'."

"Oh, well it's nice to meet ya, Marc," I slipped my hand into its partnering pocket, "well I can see an awkward moment when I smell it. Maybe we can talk later."

"Yea, maybe," Marc's eyes did all the talking. "Honey what did I tell you about strangers," I heard his voice after I began walking back towards my mother's house. Astrea didn't put up much of a fight. "You're only fifteen years old, and that man smells like he just blew in from Chester." Detroit actually. "He could be Dateline's next rapist segment..." After that I faded it out, stepping inside to the greeting mock of Dawn, who'd apparently been watching the whole time.

"That guy's wearing flannel and it's eighty-nine degrees outside," were her first words, "huh. Funny. I knew a guy like that. Had a lot to hide. Lotta secrets."

"Really," I grabbed a beer from the fridge, cracking it open over the edge of the counter, "sounds like the beginning of a rape story. Speaking of which, answer me this, how come all you women have one of those?"

"What?" And that was the end of that discussion. I woke up on the kitchen floor to what I later discovered was about five hours later, head throbbing, and broken glass all over the floor. The bitch had smashed my beer against my head. Probably in defense of my inquiry. Dean was right. Smart man, that Dean.

"People fall from grace in a similar manner that leaves fall from trees in the fall; slowly at first, with a quick detachment. Swaying here and there. But once they've landed, there's no taking off again," a high pitched voice led me from the kitchen. Like someone had their headphones turned up to an unhealthy level. I found Dawn asleep on one of the couches in the living room. And as guessed, she had these big bulky headphones strapped over her head, and had been listening to what sounded like a self-help preacher of some kind. I picked up the CD cover and read to myself: "Coping with Rape: One Woman's Struggle Against Memory". Poor thing. I didn't feel like listening to the voice in her headphones any longer, so I stepped out back to meditate. I'd read somewhere that meditation helps the meditator.

I found a semi-medium-sized moleskin notebook on the stone table close to the back door. On it was scribbled the line:

"Driving with the top down does for the hair what music does for the soul." --- S.F.

Opening the little book, I saw that the notebook belonged to Astrea, as noted by the immediate inscription: "This notebook belongs to Astrea Foster. Open this without permission and I'LL KILL YOU." Cute. But why would she leave this out on my mother's table...unless she wanted me to find it? I suppose there must have been a good reason, if not a bad one. She was fifteen. We'd just met. I was a disgusting old, mentally disfigured individual with not a goddamn penny to my name, at least none that were legitimately earned by myself. Skipping the meditation, because I was now too distracted, I returned into the house, to find the lovely Dawn back in the kitchen, cleaning up the broken glass from the bottle she'd kamikazed against my skull.

"I'm sorry, man," she said. I could only assume she was apologizing because something in those tapes she was listening to mentioned something about forgiving and forgetting. She'd certainly never apologize for anything based on her effort alone. She wasn't built that way. "I'm sorry for the bottle. Sometimes I just snap, ya know? Ya ever feel like that sometimes?"

"Well sure," I leaned over the counter, watching her sweep glass, "but I gotta give ya respect. I've wanted to smash a bottle or two against the head of an asshole or two but never had the balls to really do it. I'm kind of a pussy that way. You've got ambition."

"When I was a kid my guidance counsellor in high school called it 'misdirected passionate conviction'," she laughed at that, "When really he just didn't want to tell me my parents were a couple pieces of shit."

"Why were they pieces of shit?"

"Since when did you care?"

"Someone wise once told me that I should ask more questions verbally, instead of gawking like an imbecile waiting for the answers to automatically appear."

"Who the hell told ya that?"

"Well, I read it in a fortune cookie, so I guess technically it wasn't really someONE."

"Ha, you are an imbecile, but that's okay," she cleared her throat, finishing up the cleaning job and grabbing two beers from the fridge, handing me one, "I promise I won't do it again," she grinned, and I accepted, but only because I was thirsty. I would have gotten a beer myself, but the bitch beat me to it. "My father was never around," she started, "I never saw him much. My mother said something about him running a dog-fighting ring just outside of town. Like a fight club for dogs. One night he left to 'attend a business meeting', and he never came back. I guess he and my mother had been having worse problems than she put out there because she didn't seem to bat an eye. Years later after I moved out, she apparently developed Alzheimer's. I visited her for a weekend in attempt to make amends, because she and I never saw eye to eye on much either. Sidenote: it was then I started to sympathize with my father for leaving all those years ago. Maybe she really was that horrible of a person to live with. Who knows? But when I stayed with her that weekend, I found that her illness had progressed significantly. She would pour glass after glass of wine, swearing that she was only drinking one glass of wine a night. Her memory had gotten so bad, she couldn't remember that she'd already had a glass. I left worried. Afraid actually. But two weeks later she died. Apparently she'd gotten so drunk that she went for a drive. Probably to the fucking liquor store to get more wine. She hit a telephone pole and died instantly."

"I'm sorry I asked."

While she told the story of her mother's demise, I could have sworn I was seeing another side of her. Dawn, the emotional freak.

"Don't be sorry," she laughed, shrugging it off as if the whole thing had been a bad joke, "I'm not. Bitch was cray. If it wasn't for her, I wouldn't have turned out to be such a trashy, cunty whore. Fuck. I blame my entire career path on her negligence as a parent. Her dying in a car crash was just what the fucking doctor ordered."

Putting the matter to rest without further conversational referendum, I found myself climbing into bed early. Pulling up the sheets to my chin so that my toes stuck out at the end of the bed, I watched as the sun made its final note of farewell to the day at hand. I laid there with both hands on my chest. Biting my lower lip for no discernable reason. The room I lay in was some sort of guest room. Can't imagine my mother hosting any "guests" that liked to her enough to want to spend the night. Though, she did seem the type to put on quite a party. Fake smiles and all that.

The next morning brought good old Mr. Dean along with it. Answering a pounding at the doorbell around 7am, I opened to door to find the smug, short-statured shit in his typical suit and tie getup. Jet black shades stuck to his face, and an expectant expression aimed for my gratitude of his arrival.

"I'm bettin' you're wondering why the heck I'm here," he grinned.

"No wonder you're rich," I scratched the old crotch.

"It's Sunday you nitwit! Church! Come on, I'm drivin'."

"What?"

"Don't you remember, the list? Part of it includes you having to go to church every Sunday, now come on get dressed, throw somethin' on it doesn't have to be super neat or anything. Catholic Mass isn't exactly a black tie affair these days," he stepped into the house, pushing his way in as if he owned the house himself. "Don't give me that look," Dean laughed, of course he'd be a complete idiot if he didn't expect this. How the hell was I supposed to know it was Sunday? "You don't have to live here, champ. You're under no obligation whatsoever."

"I don't even believe in fuckin' Christ. Isn't forcing someone's religious beliefs on others illegal?"

"Hah, you must not have ever heard of the Aggressive Christianity Missions Training Corps. Long story, best not get into it right now. Google it if you get the chance. Bottom line is, it's not exactly illegal and most authorities tend to look the other way if it's kept in the family, so to speak. Catch my drift?"

I threw on the clothes I wore yesterday. Ratty shit cloths that made Dean wrinkle his nose a little. He recommended that after Mass I went to one of the hundreds of clothing outlets in the Tri-State Area and spend a couple hundred bucks on new threads. It still was kind of a shock to know that I was suddenly pocketed with all this money. Maybe I should get a new wallet, or something. Dean himself didn't say anything about getting a checking account. He simply said he had both eyes on my mother's funds and handed me a debit card. Dean said that it was the only thing I needed in my wallet.

Dawn stayed home because of course her participation in my mother's list wasn't mentioned. She hated church and all things religious, same as me. If I thought about it hard enough I think that's how we met. A religious debate in a bar somewhere in Detroit? I can't remember. Memory's shot. Not that it mattered anyway.

The ride to St. Joseph's was short. The church itself was only about three miles from my mother's house. Once we got there, Mr. Dean took the liberty of introducing me to some of the people he knew, the fellowship as some religious nomenclatures call it. Most of the people were nice, I could say. Accepting, even. Old though. Very old. I'd say eighty percent of the parish were cruising the fast lane of their golden years, dead-locked with a dead-set departure date of "very soon", if not "tomorrow". It wasn't until we made the climb up the stone steps toward the actual church building that I began to feel uneasy. Churches, and most church-like places, made my veins squirm, especially if there was a cemetery attached to its property. The Priest, Father

John Patros, looked like a much older John Stamos, except for the exclusion of anything reminiscent of what might have once been eyebrows. It was this little fact that made me want to go home immediately. John Stamos was sexy. Fucking boner-solidifying. But if I had to go to a church whose head clergyman looked like the only dude I'd ever consider gay buttsex with....no. Just...good God he had the same hairstyle and everything....no.

"Isn't there another church we can go to? Can't I choose, or something?" I whispered to Dean while we made our way up the steps to greet John Stamos.

"Not according to your mother," he mumbled back, "it'll be fine. Catholics don't bite."

"Well good morning," John Stamos' smile glimmered of hope; hope that might have otherwise been paramount during the darkest days of the Bible. King James the Fifth Version. His robes followed that tradition. White and a red and gold with patches of bronze. around his shoulders he wore a purple scarf-like drapey thing. I could tell you what it was called if I was at least half-dick-deep in with the clergy crowd. To add cathartic insult to nostalgic injury, I couldn't help but notice the skin around his knuckles. The parched flesh reminded me of something I used to get stuck washing off the chalk boards in middle school when I was really bad. "I don't recognize you, are you new?"

"Well I come and go as the Big Guy upstairs demands," Dean mused, "but this here is the son of a dear old friend of mine, who recently passed."

"Oh was she the one for whom we held the funeral service for?"

"Yes, yes, that'd be the gal, wonderful woman

she was," Dean laughed as if neutrality were a crime and he wanted to be full-blown friendly with the Padre.

"Wonderful woman indeed," John Stamos gleamed with memorial pleasantries and satirical distant stares, "so then, you are her son?"

"Randall Cunningham," I said, holding out my hand for the guy to shake.

"Randall here," Dean interjected, "is going through a bit of self-discovery, or rather REcovery. He's lived a fruitful, but quite questionable life and feels like going to church...is uh, the first step in his journey for redemption. I suggested Catholicism because it's about the only form of religion that isn't about the bullshit."

"Well," John Stamos cleared his throat as a ward against Dean's blistering use of profanity, but smiled nonetheless, welcoming my hand with a shake, "it is certainly my pleasure to welcome anyone who is serious about talking to Christ for the first time. If you'd like, we can talk in a more one-on-one fashion after Mass? I promise I won't bite."

"Well-" I started-

"That would be lovely, Father! Now if ya don't mind, I kind of want to avoid the nosebleeds. This being Mr. Cunningham's first encounter with the Lord I want him to have a proper seat!" Dean escorted me around John Stamos and into the building.

"Staying after class isn't part of the deal, bub," I muttered, following in suit as Dean dipped his dirty lawyer fingertips into the Holy Water thing.

"Father, son, and the Holy Spirit," he said to himself, motioning the signs of the cross. I did the same, but only because if I didn't I was sure to be scolded. We took a seat about four rows from the pulpit on the left side. It didn't take long to notice the pale-skinned, amber-headed magnificence two rows up on the opposite side. I spoke her name silently to myself without uttering a sound. Astrea. She didn't notice me, of course. But I noticed her. I could almost smell her. My head felt fuzzy and my knees began to tremble as an earthquake does at the beginning of its rage. Somewhere in the bowels of my gut, a cult of butterflies began making their way from the pit of my stomach and marching up the steps of my esophagus. And somewhere between my legs, the blood began to flow and pulse.

"Randy, look," Dean whispered, temporarily interrupting me from my trance, "that's Mrs. Ladly," he motioned towards an old-looking lady not yet out of her sixties about three rows up on our side, "she runs the local pet store down the road. I once had a dream the involved having sex with her in the turtle food isle while the dogs in the back of the store went on a choirous rampage. Best sex of my life, so I-"

"Why are you telling me this?"

"Just making conversation, it's what people do in church. As a member of the community I'd surely hope you-"

"Yea, but...what the hell does what you're talking about have to do with church?"

"Come on, do you really think anyone here is all that saintly? If you had let me continue the story, you'd have found out that the twist at the end was that I ended up actually doing the nasty with her. Although it ended up being behind the register after hours, and the dogs had all gone to sleep. So there were a few disappointing subtle differences, but that just goes to show. Everyone here, in this building, this gathering of saintly pursuits, has a dark side. They only put on their bullshit expressions to get their foot in the door. After they leave, it's all satanic Häagen-Dazs for days. And when they return the following Sunday, the cycle continues. I'm just trying to say, that you don't have to worry about faking it. All women jokes aside, everyone here is faking it. The only thing that matters is that you abide by the list your mother left behind."

I got the feeling he was putting forth some kind of believable effort to sound helpful. Maybe that was his intention all along; he was just...a weird guy. Fucked in the head like the rest of us.

"I want you to dance with me."

Dean kept right on mumbling about the deranged definition of equality the Catholic Church, particularly this parish in particular, while a little girl's voice opened a door for my spiritual carcass to follow through.

"Dance with me, come on," Astrea wore a white-lace, skin-tight dress, cut off just at the middle of her thighs. Her make-up was pure, and vague, and if I stared deep enough, I couldn't see it at all. And under the glow of the dimly-lit sunlight, she held me hand while leading us into a sparkly-buzzed dance hall. I felt like I was crashing my own prom again. "Now, put your arms around me."

"But-"

"Shhh," she smiled, and I melted, "it doesn't matter what anyone thinks. All I want to do is dance. Dancing doesn't lead to anything. Dancing is not the gateway drug everyone puts it out to be."

"Yea, but your father might disagree," I laughed, feeling her tiny waist with my hands. Christ. But then again...this was her idea after all. Not mine. She wanted to dance. If anyone gave us a problem, they could go fuck themselves.

When she stepped to the right, I stepped to the left. When she stepped backward, I moved in closer. Soon, what few lights passed between us became choked, until they were closed off altogether and there was only us. She was so much shorter than me, so tiny and small. I was a giant and she was a cloud. The people around us didn't seem to notice us, and that was fine. Pretty soon I didn't notice them at all, and I began to see in Astrea what she saw in me.

But suddenly, the music stopped. And we were alone. Her demeanor seemed to change with the interruption, her dress took on a darker tone. And I tore it from her skin with both hands like a beast skinning its meal. Pushing her up against the wall, she began to cry.

"Peace be with you," John Stamos roared.

"And also with you," the audience obeyed.

But I continued. I touched her breasts, grabbing them at first...and then squeezing. Tighter I clenched, until her moans made my ears hurt. In a rage, I threw her to the right and bent her forward over a desk. She didn't want to be here. She wanted to dance...but she didn't want this.

"Peace be with you," John Stamos roared.

"And also with you," the audience obeyed.

But I continued. In one hand I pulled back on her hair and with the other I slapped her ass. And with my strength, I kept her legs spread about by pressing my feet against the inside of hers...keeping her legs pried open. Her fingernails dug into the surface of the desk...splitting to her cuticles. And I slipped in...

"Peace be with you," John Stamos roared.

"And also with you," the audience obeyed.

I found myself biting my fingernails. Staring at the back of Astrea. She looked tired, like she had gone to too many Masses.

"Dancing is not the gateway drug everyone puts it out to be," her voice, her wisdom, her smile. But then...I had imagined it myself. She'd never spoken the words. She and I then would never dance. I would never feel her tiny waist. And I would never know what it felt like to be inside her.

IV. Menagerie Man

The whiskey was cold tonight. A consumable, crisp winter sunrise stuck in the bottom of my glass. Just my kind of drink. Inside, Dawn had found the diary. Thinking it was another woman's, because according to her she was the only woman allowed in my hell, she set it aflame. I never got to read page one.

There was a bookstore in town I think. I'm sure all towns had them. But I thought maybe I should buy Astrea a replacement diary. Maybe she'd like that. Seeing as though Dawn was drugged and passed out, stinking up the living room, and probably also in the process of leaving one of her famous sweat stains on the couch, if she asked later why I was gone...and only if I felt the need to avoid an argument, I decided that my motivation for leaving the house would be to find a new set of couch cushion covers. She knew she had a sweat gland issue. It wouldn't be the first time I'd replaced the covers.

It wasn't late, sometime after dinner time. Or something like around the time most people who went out to eat went out with the family. In town, I must have scared the locals. Most women upon witnessing my oncoming presence did the "look away" gesture with their children. Their husbands of course keeping eye contact with me to see if I was the sort of creature having recently escape d their nightmares. I was an out of towner. Not familiar to their focused eyes. To them, I was hopefully just someone passing through. Someone who was on their way to a completely different town far, far away from here. Hopefully their children wouldn't remember me, And then maybe they'd grow up in the same manner as their wallet-thick parents.

I was used to it.

I found a book store though. Like the town, and all the peacoat-wearing people in it, the establishment had thick, clean walls, bright lights exuding from within, in a way that welcomed all townsfolk or even outsiders of similar caliber, yet shunning all those who couldn't remember to use, or even afford a stick of deodorant. I saw my image in the glass window.

Hair greased and ill-composed. Slack shoulders. Face grimy and eyes sunken in from my afternoon booze bath. I couldn't tell you what I may or may not have smelled like, but the very breath escaping my lungs....as it pressed and fogged against the window, appeared caked with soil. Reminding myself that all I'd come here for was a little diary, I stepped in, and proceeded toward the restroom to puke up my afternoon booze bath.

"Bathroom free?" Scraggily, mean-spirited voice. An old man appeared from behind a stack of bibles. He wore a faded denim pair of slacks and a white v-neck t-shirt. The same kind my father used to wear when he mowed the lawn on Sundays. Stuck in his curled and frumpy chest hair, lay entangled a shiny gold crucifix. And on his shirt, he wore a nametag sticker reading: "HELLO MY NAME IS GRANT".

I swear I knew him from somewhere.

"Yes, except if you're name is Grant," I muttered, "All Grant's can proceed to the back alley behind the store to go fuck themselves." He shoved passed me with a psoriasis-encased arm and mumbled something in his native tongue. But his face...I knew it from somewhere...something about that gaze. It was vacant...but full. If that made any bit of sense.

I wanted to wait for him. I was just...too curious. He was a quick one though, that Grant. Before I could decide on a hiding place from which to begin my stalking, he emerged from the bathroom, gun in hand, aimed for my stomach. A gunshot went off. I collapsed to my knees, and my sight and my ears were like nothing. I could vaguely make out his form in front of me. And I could sort of hear the pounding of hurried footsteps rushing this way and that.

"It's just not your lucky day," his words were spoken as fingernails scrape a granulated cement surface, "I've had my fill of this place, and everyone in it. If I can't go back or go forward, I'll end it altogether."

"Uh..."

"Sorry, pal," he said, "I just can't go out alone. I can't die alone." He pulled the trigger again, and I fell backward. I felt pressure in my chest...and that was when I knew where he'd shot me. Right through the left lung. He then put the gun to his head, pulled the trigger, and painted the bookshelf to his immediate right red and darker shades of red.

I lay there on the floor. Not knowing what to think other than the obvious: Is this how most people die?

Unsure why.

Unfinished in their deeds.

Nothing answered.

Everything left on the slate.

Catapulted backwards and forwards

simultaneously.

Of course there was no light, or even an inkling of a light. I felt heavier, not lighter. My eyes darkened. The pain subsided. And just like that...I became nothing.

I died. And have been made all the better for it.

Death Tokes a Holiday

A Short Story

One man's lust for weed and local mythology cross paths with a new strand of marijuana, which when smoked the right way, transports the mind of the smoker through time and space into the body of any random person moments before the time of their death.

The Oak Tree on Blossom Street was four hundred years old, at least. I knew this, because a history of it was the focal point in our small town's museum that tourists came to visit. According to legend, the tree was planted by some fellow named Robert Wilson who died around 1600 by unknown causes. He was known to be an actor, magician and a clown by most. A regular prankster by others. No one really knew what happened to him before he died. Last anyone heard he was on a cargo vessel headed to China...or Africa...or some damned place. Why? Who knows? But he was never seen in Europe again alive. His body was eventually found, and covered in scars that appeared to be from whips and other torturous devices...he was also missing all his teeth.

He planted the Oak the day before he left for whatever country he went to...and made sure to have requested to be buried beneath its roots. After his body was recovered from a Cuban Trader, it was returned to his home where a funeral was held and his final wish fulfilled. As it happened... a house was built by the tree a year later. And every person who came to live at this house, "fell in love" with the tree. Likewise, in their wills, said deceased requested to be buried beneath the roots of the trees. Both full body and cremations. If you were to count every corpse buried under this tree, you'd come up with a person for just about every leaf on its branches. This was factual and known by almost everyone in my town.

There was however a second history to the tree. A sort of urban myth claimed by some rather meticulous characters in town to be closer to the truth. According to legend, rather the nearest homeless reefer addict on the corner of Main and Greensleaf, if you took any amount of quality weed, and when I say quality, I mean nothing sprayed, just good old fashioned home grown grass... , if you took any amount of quality weed and rolled it with one of the leaves of that particular Oak, in minutes, you'd be mellowed out, just like any other type of green... except following this melancholy, you'd find yourself mentally transported into the body of whoever's soul inhabited that leaf... but when they were alive near the time of their death. This homeless reefer addict was named Gustav, and claimed to be from Russia.

No one believed him...and maybe no one even tried it because according to local authorities, somehow they reached the conclusion that there wasn't a single person in town that associated with marijuana. Besides Gustav.

One day I decided to test his theory.

I walked up the street towards the corner of Main and Greensleaf. I could hear the music blasting from Gustav's stereo he had "acquired" blaring a remix of "Wipe Me Down". As I turned the corner onto Main Street, and beheld a hideous impression of the all the negroes who loved to ditty bop to the hilariously stupid song. Flailing arms and all. Gustav's shaggy mop of hair shook like a family of rusty slinkies set atop his head beneath a shabbily tied brownish red bandana. The smell in the air told me he was tripping...and by the smell, it was his own brew of the stuff. Better than "quality". I was armed with fifty bucks.

As I approached he noticed me and motioned for me to join in on his "dance".

"Come on boy, WIPE ME DOWN!" He said in a thick Russian accent. I stepped back and put my hands up in refusal. There was no way I'd be seen doing what he was doing .

"I'm only here for some weed." I asserted my intentions point blank. Gustav stopped bouncing and waving his arms like a tribesman and looked up toward me. For a minute, I thought he was going to respond angrily. But I was wrong when a conniving sneer spread across his face.

"You eh...want to see...other places....eh?" Gustav asked.

"I want to see if what you keep saying is true. But I don't want a lot. Just enough for like a ten minute trip." I asked. "I have fifty bucks." Gustav's eyes lit up.

"Nah man, first trip is free. You got a leaf?" He asked, becoming giddier and giddier. Indeed I did, I wasn't playing around. I had picked a leaf off a branch of the Old Oak on Blossom Street on the way here. I held it out. Gustav snatched it up and disappeared behind his shopping cart piled with junk of who knows what the fuck. Minutes later, he returned with the leaf rolled up with some kind of green stuff sticking out the end.

"Here's your doobie...use it wisely man. And when you get to the other side...don't be scared...you'll be back right before the end." Gustav smiled.

"Are you sure?" I asked before taking a drag.

"I do it all the time, man! Come on...wipe me down...cause I'm on!" And he continued rapping to the song that was still playing. I inhaled and instantly coughed...and I saw that Gustav couldn't help a little chuckle. But I kept inhaling, drag after drag. It was true, I was becoming more and more relaxed...and soon felt the need to sit down. Gustav was rapping away, bouncing all over the damn place like a Richard Simmons from Harlem.

And then it hit me, slowly at first...Wipe Me Down slowed to a low murmur, and Gustav's raging bouncing slowed like a movie does during an intense Matrix-style action sequence. My head fell back against the shopping cart and the sky above me spun around faster and faster. The clouds began forming faces, each one with an open mouth swallowing the one in front of it. Some clouds formed imitations of Gustav dancing around the sky, and then his arms transformed into a swarm of bumble bees that in turn morphed into the Trill Family rapping to "Wipe Me Down". And then all was black.

My shoulders ached against the teeth of a stray

chill...like waking up in your bed realizing you had a fight with the covers and they ended up on the floor. My eyes opened and I found myself in a bed. Surroundings dark as night, I reached for a lamp to turn it on... but there was none for my fingers to find. In the darkness of the room, I spied a candlestick half melted. Where was I? And then I felt someone beside me in the bed. Shifting quickly I turned over to see a woman, barely clothed...and very...oh my good lord...beautiful. Her eyes opened when I shifted and she looked at me, speaking in an English-accented voice.

"What is it? Another nightmare?" She asked. I was somewhere else. And by the look of things, in another time. I remembered the pictures in my high school history book, and made a few connections. The room was of colonial nature, fireplace on the opposite wall. "Edward?" I shook my head out of my daze and decided to play the part for now.

"Yes, sorry. I'll go back to sleep." My voice matched hers. Strong English accent. I felt like laughing, and let out a brief chuckle.

"What's so funny?" She asked flirtingly, suddenly sitting up. I laughed out loud this time. I looked over to the large window to my left. A yellow sun was beginning to rise against a lightening sky, pushing the moon and stars backward.

"You're just so beautiful." I said. But I was just playing the part. My "wife" laughed and shoved me, almost out of the bed. I grabbed her and held her arms down, and we wrestled for a few minutes. It ended with her somehow being flipped on top of me, perhaps by her own or my own plan...and she was about to kiss me when suddenly all turned to black....

SHIT!

"Was it magical?" Gustav asked. I looked around. There he was, staring down at me with a wide ass grin, eager to hear my reply. I almost felt like throwing up... but in a good way, if that made any sense.

"You asshole!" I said. "I was going to fuck her!" I cried out. At that incredibly convenient moment, there happened to bc several pedestrians passing by, who all bared witness to my outburst. I smirked and Gustav laughed to himself.

"Great stuff eh? AH!! HAHAHA!!!! But actually you weren't...remember, the trip ends just before the end of whomever you wake up inside," He winked and laughed holding his stomach. So whoever I was about to sleep with.... that woman... was going to murder... that man? "No more till tomorrow....come back tomorrow. Ya dig?" He asked. I could tell you how I begged him for more at that moment, but it would be a complete waste of time being that it only led to me going home and waiting like a kid on Christmas Eve for the morning.

Over the course of the next week, I went back once a day...paying 25 bucks a pop for a trip. I found myself in the boots of a World War II Infantryman getting ready for D-Day, and luckily returned to my own self right before we hit Omaha. On another trip I found myself upside down on a heavy metal pole being oogled at by a few dozen guys holding out dozens and dozens of dollar bills... fortunately I came to before being called into a private lap-dance session. Each trip that I took seemed to last longer than the one before it...and I was becoming addicted.

Until one day.

It had been three months since my first trip from Gustav's Famous Spiritual-Botanical Wonder. I had made a pact with myself that this would be the last trip, or at least for a while, being I'd recently found myself in a bit of a financial snafu. The credit card companies were up my ass about taking out a couple hundred dollars for buying an expensive bong. I used it to blend the Gustav strand and the Old Oak Leaves and smoke it together as such... which worked just as well.

As I wound the corner onto Main Street, there Gustav stood ...grooving around to the song "I'm Too Sexy For My Shirt". No surprise there.

"My buddy!" Gustav roared. "You come for more hit, yes?" I nodded.

"Yes. But this is the last one. I need to start paying back what I owe to other... agencies." I replied, and watched Gustav shake his head with a "I've-been-there-before" expression.

"That's shit man. Here, sit down...take a load off

eh?" Gustav handed me a freshly rolled Oak Doobie and I lit it up.

I suppose you may have been wondering how I'm able to smoke weed out in public like this. Let me just say to you that the local authorities... spend the majority of their time hanging out in their precinct locker rooms circle-jerking each other off. There is rarely a time when a cop car is seen in our town. I saw some poor woman being attacked, and would probably end up being our town's next rape victim, the other day in a small alley for Christ's sake. I couldn't do much, the rapist was big and of the thick caramel persuasion ...I'm just a little guy. He'd have snapped my head from my shoulders and popped it like a grape. Maybe turning my head and looking the other way made me an asshole... or even part of the problem in this world. To tell you the truth, the greater part of me just did not care. Apathy had taken hold of me after the endless years lived in this town.

Anyway, I smoked up and waited for the euphoria to gloriously take over. And the last thing I heard was Gustav saying something like "I'm too sexy for my hat..."

When I awoke from the temporary mental displacement, I heard screaming, of the most brutal type. In Chinese. What? There was a crack of a whip and my back stung.

"AH!" I cried out. Another crack, followed by a hundred more. Pretty soon I became used to the stinging and just winced at each searing cut. I looked up as a heavily built Chinese...General as It appeared knelt down to my level.

"Now...Mr. Wilson, where is my daughter?" He said in rough oriental-spiced English. Mr. Wilson...wait a second. Did he mean Roger Wilson?

"What are you talking about?" I gasped out. My voice was old and ragged, like that of an elderly man. My body felt as though it would fall apart upon contact from anymore lashings.

"During the show...you made her really disappear. And now she's gone! I ASK AGAIN...WHERE IS MY DAUGHTER?" He demanded...spitting into my face. I don't know what it was, but I guess some amount of memory from Roger Wilson's brain had merged with mine and I suddenly knew what was going on.

The history books at school hadn't said much. Only hinted at a bit of romance behind the scenes. But now, with these memories somehow rising to the surface... I was given more than just a brief high school history lesson.

Roger Wilson had gone to China in search of a sort of pen pal he'd had over the years. In her letters, the girl Wei had said her father was having her beaten and raped every day in exchange for peaceful relations with a neighboring war-like trade organization. Wilson had agreed that when possible, he'd go to China and rescue her through a planned magic act... making her appear to disappear, and then leave the country with her. The only problem being, something went wrong and the trap door that Wei was supposed to safely fall through, locked ...and there was no way to get her out. No one knew where she'd "disappeared" to, and for all Roger knew, Wei was still trapped in the floor.

But then I realized something, Roger's body was found toothless, and dead. He didn't escape. He didn't succeed in rescuing Wei. There'd been no record of such an event. Oh shit. Why wasn't the drug wearing off? What the hell? WHAT THE HELL?!?!

"I will ask one more time and then I will make sure you never speak again. Where is my daughter?" I looked into the General's face, and then spat at him. He wiped the mucus away and then stood up and nodded to his men.

What happened next was the most painful experience in my life... by all regards. I was placed on my back and tied down so tight, I could barely breathe. My mouth was then held open and I saw out of the corner of my eye, a hooded man reach deep in the back of my mouth with some form of medieval pliers. The metal device tightened around one of my molars and jiggled a little. There was a sickening crack and a suction amplified by myself screaming in agony. Out popped the tooth. The first of many. The only luck I had was that Roger at this point in his life was fairly old, and his teeth were not at all in their best shape. Most of them gave way easily out of the jaw. This of course was still not pleasant, and didn't make anything any nicer for the experience...but it made me happy to know that it was not my mouth. Still, why hadn't the drug worn off?

The last tooth was pulled and my mouth filled with a deep crimson. I was almost choking on it. I spat upward in agony. I turned my head over and saw that my teeth had been placed in a wooden bowl of sorts. The Chinese General held his hands behind his back and smiled.

"One last chance, Mr. Wilson. Or we take your heart," he said. Of course I refused, that was what Wilson would have done anyway. For some reason these Chinese experts felt the need to remove my heart from my back...so they had to untie me to turn me over. Big mistake on their part. As old as Roger Wilson was, he was still strong...and despite my immense pain, I was able to grab a hold of one of the hooded men, and twist his neck in one swift motion, breaking it. The General was equipped with a handgun, but I kicked it away and recovered it...pointing it at him. I don't know why I didn't shoot...perhaps it was because I wanted some leverage in case I couldn't recover Wei and escape. So I just knocked him out with a swift blow to the head. I was going to escape. I was going to find Wei. I wasn't going to let Roger Wilson die a horrible death.

But still, why hadn't the drug worn off?

Nonetheless, outside of the torture chamber...I found myself behind the curtains, behind a stage as it seemed. From somewhere, I heard scattered chatting in Chinese...probably guards. I knew where the trap door was...from Roger's memory. I burst through the curtains and took the two guards by surprise. Before they could reach for their side arms, I ended them.

And there in front of me was the trap door where Wei should have been.

My head was feeling dizzy...was the drug wearing off? At this point I was hoping that it wouldn't yet. I had to save Wei. I had to. I knelt down by the trap door and pulled it as hard as I could. Locked still. I shot the lock with the gun and splinters flew. Lifting the door, I looked down to find a woman... though, she wasn't moving.

"Wei!" I cried out. And then I said something in Chinese. "Are you ok?" I didn't know how to speak Chinese. But Roger did.

She didn't move. "WEI!"

"Stand up, Mr. Wilson." It was the General. Stupid me. I shouldn't have let him live. I slowly looked up. There was a handgun pointed at the center of my chest.

"I shouldn't have let you live." I muttered.

"Likewise, Mr. Wilson." And the gun fired, bullet piercing through my chest and out the other side. I flew back, but as I did I fired the gun I held at the General. He fell backwards as well, and when he landed on his back...a slow pool of blood began emerging from the side of his head. The General was dead. I looked over, and saw Wei, pulling herself out of the pit.

"Roger!" She cried. "No..." she said in Chinese. Her face was littered with scars and bruises.

"It's ok," I replied in Chinese, "You're alive. You're ok...take this gun...and ...there's a cargo vessel leaving tonight back to my home ...you can make it..."

The drug never wore off. My eyes grew heavy and the last thing I saw was Wei's tear-filled eyes looking into mine. The drugs never wore off...I never returned to my original body. As far as I know, Gustav just thought I was on one long trip. For all I knew, my body was still there, to become part of his collection of stuff. I would never know, because I died in someone else's body. I found myself forever trapped in a swirling, face-swallowing funnel of clouds that would never disperse.

Gustav looked at the boy's body curiously and poked at it. It had been hours upon hours since his friend took a hit. Suddenly, the boy's body leapt up and his face began sweating.

"Jesus!" Gustav fell back onto his ass.

"I'll never tell you anything you bastard!" The boy cried out. He was suddenly taken aghast at the sound of his voice. "What has happened? What accent is that you speak with? Wait...where am I? This is not the room I was just in. Why do I not feel the lashings?" He asked in swift words. Gustav looked at the boy and his face grew worried.

"Oh shit son...you...you're not him," Gustav said. The boy looked at Gustav as he stood up.

"Where am I?" The boy asked. Gustav scratched his head. He wondered, was it possible for both consciences to switch places? It was true, Gustav had never seen someone smoke as much on a consistent basis as this boy...including himself. Perhaps it was all a new effect. Some kind of evolutionary thing. Either way, there was bound to be a way to have fun with this. Gustav smiled and in a cheery Russian accent spoke.

"My boy, would you like a smoke?"

Before we continue...a "half-time", if you will:

Out of everyone I've ever had the pleasure (or displeasure, after all you can't please everyone) of sleeping with, there have been maybe...2 or 3 out of every 10 whom I could consider having at the very least felt some amount of love towards. And yes, it may have only lasted for the duration of said poon-pounding, but does that make it any less true? Does it make it any less real? How many times have you fucked any given person and silently thought to yourself: "I love you"...but when it comes time to actually saying those words, how often are those words as genuine as the moment you originally conceived them? What exactly constitutes this for everyone? Because everyone is different, obviously, but obviously everyone who has yet to tap into the possibility that love is the pinnacle of emotion, be it temporary or conducive, and nothing more than a gap that is filled by the mind and NOT by the heart, everyone who has yet to consider that...what makes it any more potent for them?

~MEANDERINGS~

On Wine

An Extended Promissory Ode

Too often do we forget life's little pleasantries. Wine of course not being anything little, but perhaps overlooked. And being that I am in fact accompanied by a glass of wine, staring at one screen being this one, and the other being the open laptop in which most if not all of my literary conception takes place...I might as well write a few words about my deep and unscrupulous, and perhaps biblical love affair I've been having with....wine...

I've just caught myself in a bit of a snafu...having started a conversation with a woman with a line exactly as follows after her wondering why we haven't talked in an indiscernible length of time: "I'd say let's be butt buddies, but I'm a virgin and afraid to lose it to a woman."

Of course I'm not a virgin, at least to some things valued as centerfolds in outlandish cultures half-across the world, like needle-dicking your neighbor's mother with a sheep-sheer, however, I find that, metaphorically perhaps, if the wine were any thicker, I'd have more shart-related bragging rights than a camel with down-syndrome. Wine truly is the juice of the Gods, and I implore everyone to acquire a hobby in which wine is a prerequisite.

And while the aforementioned is one of the few negative obscurities invoked by the juice of the Gods, it is not nearly enough to cancel out the infinitely positive POSITIVE aspects. .....

Not only does wine awaken the urge to purge a vaginal interchange with one's own testosterone-cursed trajectory, but it also gives birth to a new meaning to the word: "inspiration". All out war in the bedroom may be shortsighted and splintered if not for the promise of queef-blasted defiance, and in the respect of Judas...betray ALL expectations. Pour a glass. Forget the blank page. Summon the opposite sex. And make her one hell of a steak dinner w/ a pasta side dish. Then look them deep in their eyes, and don't say a word....(unless they're the insecure type and have no idea why the hearth is ablaze with romance-soaked flames of euphoria, in which case, get the fuck out of there before you find yourself stuck with a Stage-Potato Stalker)....don't say a word until your lips come staggeringly desperate for proximital enclosure...and THEN....pour another glass. You need to make the night last...not buckle and crumble with one single fucking kiss.

Wine can do many things whiskey cannot...for instance...THE ABOVE. At least for me. Whiskey is good for writing. Wine is good for thinking about writing and then turning to fucking the first name in your contacts list in your cell. It's clockwork. Genius clockwork.

They say life isn't fair...I say it IS fair. It's always fair. You get what you deserve...and if you fail to employ genuine romance...you GET WHAT YOU DESERVE.

Wine and dine someone today. Tonight. Tomorrow. Tomorrow night. Now. Just do it with honesty. Wine never lies, and neither should you.

Psithurism Is Not a Sound, but a Relationship;
Love Is Not a Privilege, but an Inheritance

A Thought On Love

The following disquisition is best read while listening to a playlist consisting of sensually thematic tunes, preferably with a hint of oriental eroticism...if you cannot find anything with those flavors, anything by Enya will do. Trust me, the right music can make even the most lackluster of stimulation seem like a self-guided tour of Elizabeth Taylor's formative years. A bottle or two of wine can't hurt either.

There are some things better left unsaid, some dreams unrealized, some people untouched and unkissed. And every "once upon a setting sun", a question deserves to remain unanswered, as if the very mystery itself were a romantical panty-peeler. But in the sporadically-profound words of the quasi-overrated Ernest Hemingway:

"......the sun also rises."

When was the last time you woke up on any given morning, opened your eyes and through the soaking sunrise realized you were simply a figment simpatico with that of some grand universal scheme set into motion by a nameless dreamer searching for the one true definition of "love"? Absolution may be a rite of passage, but there is no certainty if there's simply an inkling of an attraction based on curiosity, lust, and the unknown...otherwise known as the ugly stepsister of "Love"; I've found that it's not only essential to know the difference, but it is imperative to have dipped neck-deep into both with the threat of a drowning death draped across one's shoulders.

A kiss, widely seen as little more than a momentary pact made between lovers, is sometimes further short-sighted by the more materially-bound individual. Because a kiss does not always have to connect two pairs of lips, quivering and fate-bound as they may seem. No, a kiss, as gentle as a snowflake touching down after a long, knuckle-cracking descent, is quite possibly the beginning of love. Of course, if one is to understand the concept of love, the wise wanderer would dare not ignite one's self with the incinerating burden of limitations. In the same manner as children have no knowledge of time, love has no relationship with limitation.

I've kissed many a woman, felt the warmth of pursed-lips innumerable. I've looked into the eyes of both the innocent and the damned, of the tired and the damaged. I've cradled the hands of those who might for all I've been convinced to believe, have no need for something as deep and fathomless an abyss as "love" or even, dare I say, forgiveness. These hands...things fingers...these lips; they're merely tools to conceptualize and massage and form and carve out the makings of a perfect night lost in the embrace of the opposite sex. From an inlooker's point of view, there may be a considerable amount of judgment to be inflicted against my cause; however, even I know physical pleasures are scalded by limitations when "Love" is on the horizon. Love is a journey, my dear friend; love is tragic and romantic, enlightening and frantic...and it does not come without trial and error, the occasional travesty, and sacrifice. And from what I've discovered through my own personal hiraeth, is that the eyes may be the windows to her all-but derelict soul, but the lips are the stronghold imprisoning that which aspires to be her heart; a kiss may very well free even the deepest surrenderer from that asylum which they've given birth to themselves.

In the face of all this, I do not mean to impose that a

kiss itself is a symbol of love, but perhaps the scent of something more...the wind cascading between open mouths when coupled with two pairs of ocular chrysanthemums, a reminder that time does not govern the townships of the soul or for that matter, the loins; mayhaps that is a worthy representation of that crippling bridge. However, as aforementioned, love is a journey, more importantly a one-way journey; there will always be one more drop of blood to shed. With every morning I've been lucky enough to abhor, I can only hope for more to learn, even if the torrential winds responsible for Love be coexistent alongside currents of heartbreak; after all, there is a purpose for everything, and Time is merely a crutch.

And so, in the words of my most recent therapist, whose whereabouts remain unknown:

"...love is not a privilege, but an inheritance."

An Allusion to the Illusion of Seasonal Allergies...and some Hemingway for good measure

A Moveable Hemingway

“When spring came, even the false spring, there were no problems except where to be happiest. The only thing that could spoil a day was people and if you could keep from making engagements, each day had no limits. People were always the limiters of happiness except for the very few that were as good as spring itself.”

— *Ernest Hemingway, A Moveable Feast*

I’m not really sure what to make of Hemingway anymore. His work, at least what I’ve come to swallow, is very hit or miss. Take most everyone’s favorite book to burn, The Old Man and the Sea. I wanted to fucking suicide myself when my English teacher, Mrs. Beans (don’t even get me started on the caliber of torture we put her through on the basis of her name alone) handed each of us a copy of this book. Really; I’d heard enough horror stories about it that by the time I was told part of my grade depended on sifting through the proverbial hogwash of a writer with more self-entitled literary endowment than myself, I was ready to take the risk of actually failing the class just to satisfy my then somewhat pubescent rebellious lust. Much later in life, however, I was able to read it again and marveled at its simplicity, yet very true complex study of more than just what the title offers.

However, I’ve yet to really truly find a reason to respect Hemingway’s work; it’s just not my flavor, and personally I don’t see what the big deal is about him. This might sound self-defeating, as I myself am flirting with a glass full of Jameson as I write this very sentence. And as all us writers know, a liquid-enhanced ego is not always as tasteful as we presume it to be.

The aforementioned quote, albeit a bit wordy and round-about, stung me just the right way. And while I absolutely loathe everything there is that exists Springtime-related, mainly due to my biased hatred of my allergies, these musings throttled my loins especially:

"...if you could keep from making engagements, each day had no limits."

This does not apply to just springtime alone, or whatever it was Hemingway had been thinking about at the time of spewing this passage. People seem to limit themselves like clockwork; whether it be out of a falsified sense of security or by habit or by curse...people will forever be tormented by the unavoidable mental flytrap of thinking they have to stick by limiting themselves if they are to survive. The saddest part being most of those people acknowledge the presence of their limits, but have never actually considered the alternative lifestyle that bases itself quite poetically on the philosophy of limiting those limits. Having such a narrow mindset, they might as well kill themselves now and get it over with. We all die in the end anyway, so if you aren't going to take advantage of life's testicles, then why not?

I hate springtime; the allergies, the bees, the hornets, the pansies, the weeding, the neighborhood brats that seem to have a serious lack of parenting about their asses; hell, even the sky takes on a shade of blue I'd rather not be acquainted with. Easter; the celebration of Zombie Jesus. Baseball. The Philadelphia Sillies and their worse-than-dirt "fans". The HEAT....oh the HEAT. I'm an Autumn Man, full of Fall, I even bask in the occasional snowfall in nothing but m'panties...but spring...NO. Just NO.

The only thing I can say about spring, to sheepishly tie everything together into one massive knot of bullshit for this episode of Dave Matthes' Brain on Whiskey and Love, and other Drugs, is that springtime always seems to bring about a sense of renewal. Those tragedies we may or may not have had to endure during the dead of winter, making us feel weighed down to the earth and thus limiting our strength to go on...springtime, even the smell of the very air, seems to remind me that everything is going to be okay...

...assuming I can get through spring of course.

Ernest, whatever your drug of choice was during the nights you shat out the literary feast that became *A Moveable Feast*, forget about the seasons...focus on the sinister super glue keeping our limits attached to our hearts; but then again...love is a road paved with upward-facing thumb tacks lined with liquid hot magma.

Dave Matthes was born and raised in Swedesboro, New Jersey. He has attended various colleges for computer engineering, automotive science and criminal justice-like degrees, though he is mostly self-educated in the subjects of World History, Philosophy, Political Science and Spirituality. During the day, he works as a service technician and system installer for the restaurant industry.

He is a writer of prose and story-driven poetry and is the author of autobiographical books "The Slut Always Rides Shotgun", its sequel "The Passive Aggressors", the novels "In This House, We Lived, and We Died", and "Sleepeth Not, the Bastard" and volumes of poetry "The Kaleidoscope Syndrome: An Anthology", "WANDERLUST and the Whiskey Bottle Parallel", "Strange Rainfall on the Rooftops of People Watchers" and most recently the novels that make up "The Mire Man Trilogy".

Dave presently lives in Woodbury Heights, New Jersey.

To keep up to date with the current and future writings of Dave Matthes, and other nooks and crannies of his sliver of life, find him online at:

www.Goodreads.com
https://www.facebook.com/davematthesauthor
Twitter: @Boozie_Smoocher
SnapChat: boozie_smoocher
Instagram: WhiskeySlut_Remedies

Printed in Great Britain
by Amazon

68947397R00128